D1030916

English
Lyric Poems

GOLDENTREE BOOKS

C. DAY LEWIS

EDITOR

English
Lyric Poems

1500–1900

New York

APPLETON-CENTURY-CROFTS, Inc.

Published in Great Britain
under the title

A BOOK OF ENGLISH LYRICS

Acknowledgments

The editor makes grateful acknowledgments to the following for permission
to use copyright material:

The Clarendon Press, Oxford, for a poem from *The Shorter Poems of
Robert Bridges;* the Author's Literary Trustees and The Society of Authors
for poems by Walter de la Mare; The Macmillan Company of New York for
poems by Thomas Hardy from *Collected Poems;* the Oxford University Press
for poems from *The Poems of Gerard Manley Hopkins;* Holt, Rinehart &
Winston, Inc., for poems by A. E. Housman; Robert Graves and Doubleday &
Co. Inc., for poems from *Collected Poems;* for poems from *Collected Poems*
by D. H. Lawrence (Copyright, 1929, by Jonathan Cape and Harrison Smith,
Inc., 1957, by F. L. Ravagli. Reprinted by permission of the Viking Press,
Inc.); Mrs. W. B. Yeats and The Macmillan Company of New York for poems
by W. B. Yeats, from *Collected Poems.*

The editor would also like to express his gratitude to Miss Elizabeth
Collingridge for the invaluable help she has given him, in typing the anthology,
preparing the indexes, and other practical matters.

CONTENTS

v

55856

CONTENTS vii

STORY LYRICS

LYRICAL POEMS

DEVOTIONAL LYRICS

Introduction

I

A WORD, first, about the limits of this anthology. It covers four centuries, 1500 to 1900, and is confined to the poetry of Great Britain and Ireland. Many of the ballads included in the section called *Story Lyrics* were originally composed before 1500; but such ballads were not collected or printed before the seventeenth century: at the other end of our period, I have included no work by poets born after 1900. These dates are not quite so arbitrary as they may seem. Leaving aside our anonymous folk-poetry, it is fair to say that the first considerable lyricist who wrote in an English any reader today can easily understand was Sir Thomas Wyatt, born in 1503. I took 1900 as my terminal date, partly because it is difficult to get in perspective the poetry of contemporary writers, but chiefly because there is such an embarrassment of riches to choose from in the English lyric of the previous four centuries.

I have largely modernised spelling and punctuation. Something is lost by this; but more, I think, is gained. Few of us have any notion what Elizabethan English, for instance, sounded like; and most readers— particularly the younger readers for whom this book is chiefly designed —are alienated from a poem they might otherwise have enjoyed if they first meet it in the (to them) outlandish dress of archaic spelling.

The sections into which I have divided the material represent my own view of the principal uses of the lyric form, and are intended to give the book some structure. It is, of course, an arbitrary structure. For example, the lyric began as words for singing; so it seemed right to open this anthology with *Songs:* the first section offers a selection of poems which were written for music, or are familiar to us through association with well-known tunes, or to my ear have the tone and movement of song. But in the second section you will find a number of folk-songs, whose words were no less composed for singing, just as the ballads printed here were sung or musically recited. The poems in the first section are mostly what we might now call "art-songs"—madrigals, lute-songs, or poems written to be sung in plays and masques. Ballads and folk-songs sprang, not from the court, but from the common people; and, unlike the art-song, they always tell a story. That is why I have made a separate section, *Story Lyrics,* to include examples of this anonymous folk-poetry, together with some story poems written in lyrical form by poets whose names we know. Again, the dividing line between *Songs* and my third section, *Lyrical Poems,* is in some places as artificial as an international frontier, and in other places may seem virtually to disappear. A good few of the pieces I have put under *Lyrical Poems* could be sung; some of them have been set to music or even were written for that purpose: but these, to my ear, lack the simplicity or the transparency which distinguishes the true song-lyric.

Much English poetry is lyrical in quality. But mine does not set out to be an anthology of "the finest English poetry," let alone of "great poems." The strictest limitation I put upon myself in making the book was to choose no poem for it, however beautiful, seminal, well-known, unfamiliar, or what you will, which did not pass my own tests for the true lyric. These tests are personal, subjective, and possibly rather eccentric. They have been formed by my early training as a singer, by much reading of poetry, and by what I have learned from many years of writing it.

Literary criticism is not an exact science: no precision instruments exist for measuring the value of a poem—or for detecting the lyric. Subjectivism and relativism are anathema nowadays in the best critical circles; and they are indeed hazardous grounds on which to grapple with literature; but they are less hazardous—more honest and less absurd, I would even say—than is the claim of certain contemporary critics that it is now possible to assess once and for all the comparative value of poems, or the delusion of some such critics that they have done so. One need only look at the (to us) extraordinary evaluations made by highly intelligent and experienced critics in the past, to become sceptical about any method of criticism which, putting poets or poems into an order of merit, conceives them to be permanently placed. Good poems refuse to be shunted and then immobilized thus. They change places, of course; but it is time, not the critic, which sorts them out, putting some in the discard, bringing forward again now this poet, now that, as one whose work has special relevance to the needs of a present generation; just as any of us, in his lifetime, may feel a special affinity for one poet after another, receiving from each in turn a unique enlightenment about the meaning of his own experience. Today, there is a general demand for irony, for depth or complexity of meaning in poetry. This is fine—so long as we are not nudged into saying that a poem cannot be good unless it has irony in it. Anyone who holds such a view had better skip this anthology; for irony and complexity of meaning are wholly foreign to the lyric.

II

What, then, is a lyric? My dictionary defines "lyric" as "of or pertaining to the lyre; meant to be sung . . . Now the name for short poems, usually divided into stanzas or strophes, and directly expressing the poet's own thoughts and sentiments." This definition shows how impossible it is to define the lyric. For instance, it can be argued that *all* poems except dramatic ones express "the poet's own thoughts and sentiments," and on the other hand that the lyric by no means always does so "directly." Can we say that "Full fathom five" or "O sunflower weary of time" is a *direct* expression of the poet's thoughts and sentiments? Perhaps "immediate" would be a better word. A lyric can indeed convey states of mind immediately—that is, without apparent context, without argument, without comment by the poet. But this leads us into another difficulty, for many such lyrics cannot accurately be called expressions of the *poet's own* states of mind; they are pure, or they are impersonal. Pure poetry, in Mallarmé's sense of a poetry which aspires to the condition of music, is rare in English. We find it, or something near to it, in certain of Shakespeare's songs, possibly in "Kubla Khan," in a few poems by Beddoes and Christina Rossetti, in Dobell's "The Orphan's Song," in the nonsense verse of Lear and Carroll—poems from which prose meaning, rational sequence, the tendency of language to communicate through intellectual concepts, have all been excluded. Such poems either do not convey the poet's state of mind at all, or express it in so oblique and rarefied a way as to render it unimportant for the reader. What is excluded in the impersonal poem is not prose meaning and rational sequence but the poet's human individuality. The Japanese *haiku*, the poems of the Imagists, much medieval English lyric—the carols, for example—are of this nature. We can gather from them little or nothing about the personality of their writers. Whether they have "Anon" or a poet's name written beneath them, they sound equally anonymous.

Not all medieval lyrics are impersonal. But the introduction of a personal note into the English lyric was rare till Wyatt. This development was very closely connected with a major, perhaps the greatest, revolution in English poetry—the gradual detaching of the lyric from music and the establishment of it as a form in its own right. So long as lyric poems were composed to be sung, the lyric remained subordinate to the exigences of musical form; and it was also limited by conventions laying down what subjects were appropriate for song, and often by certain conventional attitudes towards these subjects. The stock subject for lyrics throughout the sixteenth century was love, and the prevalent attitudes towards it were derived from the formal code of chivalry and the Courts of Love. Here and there in this period we find a poem which breaks away from such conventional limitations. Wyatt's "They flee from me" and "My lute awake!," or Drayton's "Since there's no help," are poems in which the writer's personality thrusts through the medium—

poems which are the reverse of anonymous, and introduce a realism quite at variance with the traditions of the love song. But it is not till the end of the century that we find, in John Donne, a poet who, impatient both with the technical and the psychological fetters of lyrical tradition, consistently applied this realism to his love poetry, exploring the whole gamut of sexual feeling—its violent contradictions, its exorbitant passion, its directness and evasiveness, its idealism but also its disrespect.

Donne was seldom, in any strict sense, a lyric poet. But he and his followers won the revolution which liberated the lyric from its confinement within musical forms and Romance conventions. We can see his realism, diminished sometimes into cynicism or flippancy, in the lyrics of Caroline and Restoration poets. After Donne, a lyric could, theoretically at least, be *about* anything and written in any meter. Nevertheless, it remains true that not every state of mind, not every kind of rhythm or of language, is in practice adaptable to lyric.

Unless we throw in our hands and call any poem lyrical that is not epic, didactic or satiric, we simply must draw a line somewhere, on one side of which will be the true lyrics, on the other side a mass of hybrids possessing some lyrical quality but mixed in with qualities derived from other kinds of poetry. My own tests for the true lyric are tests of mood, rhythm, and language.

It is commonly accepted, if only in principle, that a lyric should be single-minded: it should present, that is to say, a mood or a state of mind which is unequivocal, undiluted, neither modified by intellectual reservations nor complicated by ironic overtones. It can be a cry straight from the heart ("Western wind; when wilt thou blow?"). It may be, on the other hand, a frivolous or a patently "artificial" poem, yet one which nevertheless gives an effect not only of simplicity but of spontaneity (e.g. Rochester's "Love and Life"). In other words, it is a song—a form of words which, whether written for music or no, keeps something of the immediacy or the artful artlessness that reveals its musical ancestry.

The business of the lyric is to make words sing and dance, not to make them argue, moralise, or speechify. For this reason, certain rhythms— differing in different languages—seem more natural to lyric-writing than others. In English, the heroic couplet or the blank verse line is an impossible medium for a love lyric; and the iambic pentameter, so superb an instrument for dramatic, narrative or satiric verse, so marvellously flexible, and capable (as Pope proved) of infinite subtlety even when kept to its most regular syllabic form, is a meter intrinsically—to my ear, at least—unlyrical. For this reason, I have included very few sonnets, although the sonnet form taken over by English poets from French and Italian was originally associated with music. The five-stress iambic

line seldom produces a lyrical movement; but a four- or three-stress
iambic line does, and so may a stanza in which five-stress lines are set in
a pattern with shorter ones. Why this should be so, I cannot explain. The
anapæstic rhythm sounds to me a more consistently lyrical one than the
iambic. Yet it was little used by English lyricists till the seventeenth
century, when its potentiality was shown in some of Dryden's songs.
Anapæstic rhythm, too regularly used, gives a mechanical and tedious
effect, as witness Byron's "The Destruction of Sennacherib," or certain
of Thomas Moore's *Irish Melodies* and Swinburne's poems. But a more
tactful handling of the anapæst, varying it with the iamb, can produce
a beautifully flexible lyrical rhythm—the dancing lilt we get in many
of Browning's and Hardy's shorter poems.

Finally, there is the test of language. Here I am on much more de-
batable ground. It is not difficult to recognise lyrical rhythms, or the
transparency and single-mindedness of the lyric: but is there such a
thing as lyrical language, and if so, how do we identify it? Suppose I
take a line from a poem unknown to a given reader, and ask him to tell
me, on the strength of this sample, whether the poem it comes from is
a lyric? For example,

Lo! what a mariner love hath made me!

It could come from a play or from a dramatic monologue. In fact,
it is from a poem by Surrey which I myself should call a lyrical
poem. It is wrong, of course, to base any final judgments on isolated
lines. We must consider the language of each poem as a whole, in
relation with the poem's rhythms and the purity or simplicity of the
state of mind it is expressing. Also, it would be ridiculous to suggest that
there is only one kind of lyrical language. For instance, poets have man-
aged to move far from the lyric's source in song, and write poems in a
colloquial language which nevertheless does not disqualify them as
lyrics. Yet, although I can offer no all-embracing definition of lyrical language, I seem to be able to recognise this way of saying things when I
meet it—and in lines so far removed from each other in time and subject
and intensity as Drummond's "A hyacinth I wished me in her hand" and
Heber's "By cool Siloam's shady rill."

III

Song, the source of lyrical poetry, we are apt to think of as the most
spontaneous form of literature—a welling-up of pure feeling, joyful or
sad. It was to correct this that I chose, as epigraph for my book, the lines
by a Canadian poet:

And poetry is a song, when the bird has flown,
About a bird, never the bird's own.

No amount of gush about native woodnotes wild and nests of singing birds should be allowed to conceal the fact that even a song lyric is *about* something and that, though it may be naive, no song lyric is artless. Even birds, in a sense, have to learn to sing. The verbal artifice of the Elizabethan madrigal writers is evident; but the folksong too has its conventions.

When we look at the art-songs that have survived, we can see that writing words for music need not be just a matter of writing words only viable for music. It is true that the text of many songs, like seaweed in water, does not come alive except when bathed in its element of music. But, just as Shakespeare's songs, though they are enlarged by their dramatic contexts and point their meaning, nevertheless stand firm when isolated on the pages of an anthology, so the songs of Burns have a life of their own which is not dependent upon the tunes for which they were written. Both Shakespeare's songs and Burns' are metaphors of pure, intense states of mind. There is a great distance between the deep poignancy of "Take, oh take those lips away" or "Oh wert thou in the cauld blast" and Moore's artificial sparkle. Yet Moore was not merely a superlative writer of words for music (anyone who has sung the *Irish Melodies* must pay tribute to his immaculate placing of vowel and consonant for the voice). Now and then he wrote a song like "How sweet the answer Echo makes," whose elegance and vivacity compensate for its shallowness of emotion, or one like "The Last Rose of Summer," which can teach us not to under-value sentiment nor to overlook the sincerity behind the ornateness of such lines as "And from love's shining circle The gems drop away."

The first poem in this book has a refrain—"In youth is pleasure"; and such refrains will frequently be found amongst the poems printed in the first two sections. Refrain is essential to art-songs, folksongs, and ballads. It may take the form of a repeated verbal phrase, which enabled the composer to repeat a musical phrase and thus round off the stanza and the whole song. It may be a chorus. It may be a stock opening, like the folk-singer's "As I roved out." In ballads, too, we often come upon repetitions ("He hadna gone a mile, a mile, A mile but barely three"), which were useful to the reciter as mnemonics, and gave listeners the pleasure of recognition. But verbal refrains are only one kind of repetition. There is also the recurrence of sound in rhymes, and there is the pulsing of meter. One could almost define the song lyric as a poem in which, even when there is no verbal refrain, the ear is made to expect one. All lyrical poetry reveals its origin in song, however faintly, by the sense it gives that a single theme is running and repeating itself through the variations.

As I have said, the dividing line between song lyric and lyrical poem is sometimes negligible. Herrick's "Julia" poems, for example, could come into either category. I have placed them under *Songs* because they have the simplicity of syntax which is usually desirable for a song: complex sentences are awkward for composer and singer to deal with. But this holds more generally true for the solo song than for such elaborate musical forms as the madrigal. It must also be said that all too often, particularly in collections of modern verse, we come across poems entitled "Song" which by no conceivable stretch of the imagination or the larynx could ever profitably be sung. While the liberation of the lyric form from musical dominance enabled lyrical poetry to enlarge its scope and blossom out in a variety which would have amazed the Elizabethans, we may regret that this liberation has now become a divorce, and be sorry that the Elizabethan kind of poet-composer or the close collaboration between musician and poet has gone, it seems, for good.

In *Maud* and *The Princess,* Tennyson wrote some wonderfully musical lyrics, but no composer of the first rank was available to set them with the distinction they merited. In our own century, the lyrics of A.E. Housman (a natural song-writer who was perversely hostile to the idea of his poems being put to music) received fine musical treatments from Vaughan Williams and Butterworth. And cycles of poems by Thomas Hardy, a great lover of music, have been set by Britten and by Gerald Finzi. Otherwise, the twentieth-century revival of British music has not yet made any very significant progress towards the recreation of song lyric.

IV

In an introduction to *English and Scottish Popular Ballads,* the work of that great collector, Francis James Child, G.L. Kittredge writes, "A Ballad is a song that tells a story, or—to take the other point of view—a story told in song. More formally, it may be defined as a short narrative poem, adapted for singing, simple in plot and metrical structure, divided into stanzas, and characterised by complete impersonality so far as the author or singer is concerned."

The mass of ballad material, upon which I have drawn for section two, *Story Lyrics,* was composed before the invention of printing and handed down by oral tradition, each ballad receiving accretions and modifications through the years, so that there are several variants of most of them. I have chosen, from Child's monumental work, those variants of my selected ballads which seem to me most effective both as lyric-writing and as story-telling. There can be little doubt that the authorship of these ballads was a communal one: the author-singer would take the lead in putting an episode into words, but members of his community would collaborate, and later the ballad might be carried into other villages and towns, where differing versions of it would be built up. Ballads were not communal in this sense only. They also provided for their primitive audiences a cross between the "pop-song" and the tabloid. The predominant subjects of ballad are violence, sex, and the supernatural—today the tabloid concentrates upon violence, sex and money. The ballads were popular songs because their subjects were of absorbing interest to the community, and because the composing and singing of them focused the communal spirit. They are gossip, transformed into poetry.

Our folk-songs, too, are commonly concerned with the same three subjects. They, too, are anonymous, and they tell a story, though on the whole less dramatically, more lyrically, than the ballad. What ballads and folk-songs have in common, as against the art-song, is their consistent impersonality: we get no hint of what the author himself feels about the events he is recording; and there is little emotional subtlety, less moralising or psychologising, in the narrative. Another feature most noticeable in this genre is economy. With the technique of film-cutting, the story moves from high spot to high spot, leaving out the intermediate stages: it is this, of course, together with the rangy, springy, rapid meter and the communal pressure behind them, which gives the ballads their remarkable vitality.

The invention of printing was to be, in the end, the death of this form of folk-poetry, just as it would also be partly responsible for the deplorable modern alienation between "literature" and "entertainment." However, the folk tradition died hard; and I have been able to include in *Story Lyrics* a few examples of relatively modern folk-writing—street ballads from London and Dublin, for instance, and several songs from the North-East of England ("Blaydon Races" has been called the national anthem of the North-East, and "The Plodder Seam" is one of an interesting group of mining poems collected by A. L. Lloyd). British literature, however, is by no means as rich as American in good work-songs—we have few railroad ballads or convict songs, for instance, to compare with those of the U.S.A.

Something of the tone of folk-song survives in poems by John Clare, who was a peasant, and in the Dorset dialect poems of William Barnes, a clergyman and a scholar. The ballad tradition sprang to life again when professional poets found inspiration in Percy's *Reliques*. Coleridge's *Ancient Mariner* is certainly one of the greatest poems in the

English language; but, although it is a true story-lyric, the drama it unfolds is an inner drama. Similarly, Cowper's "The Castaway," under the guise of a story about a man drowning, expressed the poet's despairing conviction that he was cut off from God and man, eternally damned; while Crabbe's extraordinary poem, "Sir Eustace Grey"—I have room for only a part of it—is a study in guilt and madness which must surely have derived from the agonies of mind the poet himself suffered as a young man.

Apart from an occasional adaptation of the old ballad manner, such as Scott's *Marmion,* and apart from a few objective lyrical works like Hardy's "A Tramp-Woman's Tragedy," the best story-lyrics of the last two hundred years have been subjective poems. "La Belle Dame Sans Merci" is no less, though less obviously, a poem about Keats' state of mind than is *The Castaway* about Cowper's. Further removed still from the old ballad, but related to it because they present action lyrically, are the dramatic lyrics of Browning and the remarkable poem with which this section ends—Robert Graves' "The Foreboding." Such is the vitality of the ballad form, so much scope does it offer a poet who wishes to tell a story, to describe a person or an episode, in a lyrical style, that it is unlikely to disappear from our literature. The ballads of W. H. Auden, William Plomer, and Charles Causley, contemporary poets, show some of the ways in which this form can be modified to suit the meanings and poetic language of today.

V

Turning to the first piece in *Lyrical Poems,* we see foreshadowed something of the ampler scope which the lyric was to attain after its detachment from music. Wyatt's "Is it possible?" has a song refrain, but lacks the regular pattern of stresses usually found in the art-song (not, of course, in folk-songs). Its language is simple, but the syntax less so— each five-line stanza is one extended sentence. Though the poem does sing, it is singing a recitative rather than an aria. Finally, the poem is thinking, soberly and seriously thinking, on a subject which most sixteenth-century poets, when they wrote lyric, were content to treat in a shallower, more conventional manner; and through these turns of thought we are made to feel the personality of the poet himself. It is interesting to compare this poem with one on a related theme—Thomas Hardy's "The Going," written when his first wife died after a gradual estrangement over many years. Wyatt's poem, comparatively, is austere, formal, abstract; Hardy's is dramatic, sensuous, flexible in its rhythms, more obviously personal and emotional. But these two poems, four centuries apart, have an affinity. Both of them approach their subject with a whole-hearted seriousness. Neither could have been written if words and music had never come together in an art form, or if poets had been unable to break this close lyrical association without poetry's altogether losing the qualities derived from it.

The most notable line of development in English lyrical verse can be traced in its power to deal seriously with a widening range of subject matter, while preserving its lyrical character. Shakespeare in his sonnets, Donne in his love poems, explored far more deeply into the meanings of experience than any of their lyric predecessors. But their deployment of thought and syntactical patterns were generally too complex for these poems to come properly within my definition of the lyric. Seriousness, depth and resonance of meaning, allied to the authentic lyrical utterance as I hear it, appear most signally in Wyatt, in Shakespeare's songs, in Marvell, in Blake's *Songs of Experience*, Wordsworth's Lucy poems, a few of Emily Brontë's, and more than a few by Hardy and Yeats. I will pass over for the moment the kind of poem included in my final section, *Devotional Lyrics*.

The lyric line appears to have considerable gaps. For instance, there was little good lyric writing between the end of the seventeenth century and the Romantics. But the eighteenth century was the great age of hymn-writing; moreover Charles Wesley, Issac Watts and other hymn-writers took over for their own purpose the four-square meter which had been so commonly used in cynical or lascivious songs by Restoration lyricists—anticipating, no doubt, the Salvation Army's sturdy refusal to let the Devil have all the best tunes. Again, the early seventeenth century for most of us means the Metaphysical poets, whose work is indeed one of the greater glories of English poetry. But its value was little recognized in their own time, and this kind of poetic thinking had too elaborate a dialectic for the lyrical mode—lyrics do not argue. We must remember, though, that while Herbert, Vaughan, Crashaw and other followers of Donne were writing, there were also lyrical poets at work, who were sometimes influenced by the great Metaphysicals and now seem overshadowed by them. Carew, Waller, Davenant, Suckling, Lovelace, for example, wrote lyrics the best of which have outlived their day.

The verse of the Cavalier poets and the Restoration lyricists may not much appeal to modern readers, who look for irony, tough thinking, sincerity, a roughened surface. These poets, with their smoothness, their rather facile paradoxes and antitheses, their apparent frivolity of attitude, must evidently be rated as minor writers. But I am not myself disposed to reject lyrics which are technically so accomplished, which run easily, and display such verve, urbanity, or high spirits as those of Dryden, Rochester, Sedley, Gay. "Poetry does not have to be great or even serious to be good," said W. H. Auden in his inaugural lecture at Oxford. Anyone who has to work his way through the mass of minor verse produced in the nineteenth century may well regret the loss of that urbane poise and gaiety we find in Restoration lyrics. Pope and his followers made little use of the lyric form: the Romantics used it for serious purposes. We can see the break most easily in Hood, who wrote some excellent lyrics but kept his lighter side for facetious, punning verse, and never the twain did meet. We have no Victorian writer, except Clough in a few passages of *Amours de Voyage*, who manages to be at once lyrical and amusing. The great Romantics certainly enlarged the scope of the lyric, as they enlarged human sensibility. Very few earlier lyrics have the resonance of Wordsworth's "A slumber did my spirit seal," or even of Keats' "In a drear-nighted December" (I have not included any of his Odes, since they lack the singleness of mood which I take as one of the essentials of true lyric; they are, of course, altogether greater works than those of his I have printed here). But the spiritual pressure behind their finest lyrics was never equalled by their immediate successors. With the Victorians, the Romantic seriousness dwindled into solemnity and all too often into mawkishness. The Victorians did, however, extend the lyric in two directions: the detailed observation of nature—we get this from Tennyson, and Browning, from Patmore, D. G. Rossetti and Meredith, above all from Hopkins—and the lyrical treatment of human relationships on more intimately personal lines than poets had cared to attempt before.

VI

My last section, *Devotional Lyrics*, is necessarily thinner. There have been only two notable phases of religious poetry in England. First, that of the carols, most of which were made between 1400 and 1647, when the Puritans clamped down on Christmas. The carols, like the ballads, are largely anonymous, and they came from the same source. The "Cherry-Tree Carol," for instance, has all the features of folk-poetry which we find in the ballad. At its best, in "I sing of a maiden," this early religious verse shows an incomparable purity. Many of the carols, with their blend of innocence and earthiness, Christian doctrine and pagan vivacity, their Latin tags and peasant naïveté, have lyrical merit. But they live less fully on the page, separated from the tunes with which we associate them, than do other kinds of folk-poetry. So I have included only a few of them.

The second phase, which came at the end of the period in which the carol flourished, is that of Donne, Herbert, Vaughan, Crashaw, Traherne. These poets were all, in their different ways, exploring deeper into religious experience than any of their predecessors. The lyric medium was seldom adequate for such exploration, and no doubt the religious dissensions of their time made an unclouded lyrical simplicity all the more difficult to achieve. The three greatest English religious poets are Donne, Herbert and Hopkins, but I have included no poem by Donne or Hopkins in this section, for their religious poetry seems to me outside the limits of the lyric. However, the other Metaphysicals, for all their tough thinking and intricate verbal texture, did occasionally produce simpler devotional poems which I can thankfully admit to this collection.

When we turn to the eighteenth-century hymn-writers, it is interesting to find in Cowper's "God moves in a mysterious way" a brilliant use of the Metaphysical conceit, modified so as not to impede the straight-forward movement of the poem's theme. These writers, whether as supporters of the Establishment they deprecated "enthusiasm" or as dissenters they encouraged it, alike show reflected in their hymns the eighteenth-century balance and elegance: good sense is not, on the face of it, a very promising ingredient for devotional poetry; yet the best hymns of this period strike one not only with the note of piety but as eminently sensible and forthright too. In his noble poem, "The spacious firmament on high," Addison was able to say of the stars, without any incongruity or pedantry, "In *reason's* ear they all rejoice."

Where English devotional poetry falls short is in the lack of a great mystical poet. Neither Donne, Herbert, nor Hopkins was a mystic. Crashaw comes a little nearer, perhaps. But the only first-rate mystical poetry I know, in the sense of poetry that conveys to us some inkling of the mystical experience, is the stanzas I have included from Emily Brontë's "The Prisoner." It was the lack of this (extremely rare) inner fire which prevented Christina Rossetti from becoming a devotional poet of the highest rank. She possessed a versatility and technical skill in the use of varied stanza forms comparable with George Herbert's; but she had little of his power to concentrate thought in a firmly-woven yet lucid pattern—his elegance of mind, and the good manners which, as A. Alvarez has perceptively noted, he brought to poetry. Her religious verse, though far from negligible, is too often diffuse, pietistic, even sentimental. She never achieves those deep penetrations into the reality of religious experience which we find occasionally in the work of her American contemporary, Emily Dickinson.

❋   ❋   ❋

The poems within each section follow one another roughly in the
birth order of the poets who wrote them; but I shifted some about a bit,
while maintaining a general sequence of "periods" and "schools," if I
felt they could thus make congenial links with neighbors not quite of
their own time. Those who are keen on dates will find the poets dated in
the Contents. A few famous and indisputably lyrical poems (Meredith's
Love in the Valley, for example) I have had to leave out on the score of
length; and I confidently expect readers to upbraid me about other sins
of omission—and indeed of commission. An anthology which should
satisfy everyone is not only impossible, it would also be insufferable. I
should like this one to make readers argue as well as enjoy. I have given
them, both in my arrangement of the material into sections, and in
certain provocatively dogmatic passages of this Introduction, plenty to
quarrel about. But I beg the reader to realize that definitions of the
lyric, divisions of lyrical poetry into this and that and the other, placing,
historicising, and all the other critical enterprises, are marginal activi-
ties. "A poet at least thinks a poem more important than anything which
can be said about it"—and so should every reader, whether or no he be
a critic, particularly if he *is* a critic. If this book has done something to
show the range and vitality of a poetic form that is today a little out of
fashion, and if it persuades the reader to push it aside and turn to the
whole work of poets given here only in samples, then it will have served
its purpose.

C. DAY LEWIS

SONGS

And poetry is a song, when the bird has flown,
About a bird, never the bird's own.

ROBERT FINCH

"In an arbour green"

In an arbour green, asleep whereas I lay,
The birds sang sweet in the middes of the day;
I dreamed fast of mirth and play:
    In youth is pleasure, in youth is pleasure.

Methought I walked still to and fro,
And from her company I could not go;
But when I waked it was not so:
    In youth is pleasure, in youth is pleasure.

Therefore my heart is surely pight
Of her alone to have a sight,
Which is my joy and heart's delight:
    In youth is pleaure, in youth is pleasure.

ROBERT WEEVER

pight = fixed

"Art thou gone in haste?"

Art thou gone in haste?
    I'll not forsake thee!
Runn'st thou ne'er so fast,
    I'll o'ertake thee!
O'er the dales or the downs,
    Through the green meadows,
From the fields, through the towns,
    To the dim shadows!

All along the plain,
    To the low fountains;
Up and down again,
    From the high mountains:
Echo, then, shall again
    Tell her I follow,
And the floods to the woods

Carry my holla.
Holla!
Ce! la! ho! ho! hu!

ANON.

"*My lute awake!*"

My lute awake! perform the last
Labour that thou and I shall waste,
  The end that I have now begun;
For when this song is sung and past,
  My lute be still, for I have done.

As to be heard where ear is none,
As lead to grave in marble stone,
  My song may pierce her heart as soon;
Should we then sigh or sing or moan?
  No, no, my lute, for I have done.

The rocks do not so cruelly
Repulse the waves continually,
  As she my suit and affection,
So that I am past remedy;
  Whereby my lute and I have done.

Proud of the spoil that thou hast got
Of simple hearts thorough love's shot,
  By whom, unkind, thou hast them won,
Think not he hath his bow forgot,
  Although my lute and I have done.

Vengeance shall fall on thy disdain
That makest but game on earnest pain;
  Think not alone under the sun
Unquit to cause thy lovers plain,
  Although my lute and I have done.

Perchance thee lie withered and old
The winter nights that are so cold,

Perchance = it may be

Plaining in vain unto the moon;
Thy wishes then dare not be told;
  Care then who list, for I have done.

And then may chance thee to repent
The time that thou hast lost and spent
  To cause thy lovers sigh and swoon;
Then shalt thou know beauty but lent,
  And wish and want as I have done.

Now cease, my lute: this is the last
Labour that thou and I shall waste,
  And ended is that we begun;
Now is this song both sung and past:
  My lute be still, for I have done.

                              SIR THOMAS WYATT

Of His Cynthia

Away with these self-loving lads,
Whom Cupid's arrow never glads!
Away, poor souls, that sigh and weep
In love of those that lie asleep!
  For Cupid is a meadow god,
  And forceth none to kiss the rod.

Sweet Cupid's shafts, like destiny,
Doth causeless good or ill decree.
Desert is born out of his bow,
Reward upon his wing doth go.
  What fools are they that have not known
  That Love likes no laws but his own!

My songs they be of Cynthia's praise,
I wear her rings on holidays;
In every tree I write her name,
And every day I read the same.
  Where honour Cupid's rival is,
  There miracles are seen of his.

If Cynthia crave her ring of me,
I blot her name out of the tree.

If doubt do darken things held dear,
Then well fare nothing once a year!
  For many run, but one must win;
  Fools, only, hedge the cuckoo in.

The worth that worthiness should move
Is love, that is the bow of Love.
And love as well the foster can
As can the mighty nobleman.
  Sweet saint, 'tis true you worthy be,
  Yet without love nought worth to me.

     Sir Fulke Greville, Lord Brooke

foster = forester

"*And can the physician . . .?*"

And can the physician make sick men well?
And can the magician a fortune divine?
Without lily, germander, and sops-in-wine,
     With sweet-briar
     And bon-fire
     And strawberry wire
     And columbine.

Within and out, in and out, round as a ball,
With hither and thither, as straight as a line,
With lily, germander, and sops-in-wine.
     With sweet-briar
     And bon-fire
     And strawberry wire
     And columbine.

When Saturn did live, there lived no poor,
The king and the beggar with roots did dine,
With lily, germander, and sops-in-wine.
     With sweet-briar
     And bon-fire
     And strawberry wire
     And columbine.

          Anon.

"Whenas the rye"

Whenas the rye reach to the chin,
And chopcherry, chopcherry ripe within,
Strawberries swimming in the cream,
And schoolboys playing in the stream;
Then, O, then, O, then, O, my true love said,
'Till that time come again
She could not live a maid.

GEORGE PEELE

"Gently dip"

Gently dip, but not too deep;
For fear you make the golden beard to weep.
Fair maiden white and red,
Comb me smooth, and stroke my head:
And thou shalt have some cockle bread.
Gently dip, but not too deep,
For fear thou make the golden beard to weep.
Fair maiden, white, and red,
Comb me smooth, and stroke my head;
And every hair, a sheaf shall be,
And every sheaf a golden tree.

GEORGE PEELE

A Sonnet

His golden locks time hath to silver turn'd;
O time too swift, O swiftness never ceasing!
His youth gainst time and age hath ever spurn'd,
But spurn'd in vain; youth waneth by increasing.
　Beauty, strength, youth, are flowers but fading seen,
　Duty, faith, love are roots, and ever green.

His helmet now shall make a hive for bees,
And, lovers' sonnets turn'd to holy psalms,
A man at arms must now serve on his knees,

And feed on prayers, which are age his alms.
  But though from court to cottage he depart,
  His saint is sure of his unspotted heart.

And when he saddest sits in homely cell,
He'll teach his swains this carol for a song,
Blest be the hearts that wish my sovereign well,
Curst be the souls that think her any wrong.
  Goddess, allow this agèd man his right,
  To be your bedesman now, that was your knight.

GEORGE PEELE

"Love is a sickness"

Love is a sickness full of woes,
  All remedies refusing;
A plant that with most cutting grows,
  Most barren with best using.
      Why so?
More we enjoy it, more it dies;
If not enjoyed, it sighing cries,
      Heigh ho!

Love is a torment of the mind,
  A tempest everlasting;
And Jove hath made it of a kind
  Not well, nor full, nor fasting.
      Why so?
More we enjoy it, more it dies;
If not enjoyed, it sighing cries,
      Heigh ho!

SAMUEL DANIEL

Damelias' Song to His Diaphenia

Diaphenia like the daffadowndilly,
  White as the sun, fair as the lily,
    Heigh ho, how I do love thee?

I do love thee as my lambs
Are belovèd of their dams,
   How blest were I if thou would'st prove me?

Diaphenia like the spreading roses,
That in thy sweets all sweets encloses,
   Fair sweet how I do love thee?
I do love thee as each flower
Loves the sun's life-giving power,
   For, dead, thy breath to life might move me.

Diaphenia like to all things blessèd,
When all thy praises are expressèd,
   Dear joy, how I do love thee!
As the birds do love the spring,
Or the bees their careful king:
   Then in requite, sweet virgin, love me!

HENRY CONSTABLE

"Tell me, where is fancy bred?"

Tell me, where is fancy bred,
Or in the heart, or in the head?
How begot, how nourishèd?
   Reply, reply.

It is engendered in the eyes,
With grazing fed; and fancy dies
In the cradle where it lies.
   Let us all ring fancy's knell.
   I'll begin it. Ding, dong, bell.
   Ding, dong, bell.

SHAKESPEARE

"Sigh no more"

Sigh no more, ladies, sigh no more,
   Men were deceivers ever;
One foot in sea, and one on shore,

To one thing constant never.
   Then sigh not so,
   But let them go,
And be you blithe and bonny,
Converting all your sighs of woe
Into Hey nonny, nonny.

Sing no more ditties, sing no mo
   Of dumps so dull and heavy
The fraud of men was ever so,
   Since summer first was leavy.
   Then sigh not so,
   But let them go,
And be you blithe and bonny,
Converting all your sighs of woe
Into Hey nonny, nonny.

SHAKESPEARE

"Under the greenwood tree"

Under the greenwood tree
Who loves to lie with me,
And turn his merry note
Unto the sweet bird's throat,
Come hither, come hither, come hither:
   Here shall he see
   No enemy
But winter and rough weather.

Who doth ambition shun
And loves to lie i' the sun,
Seeking the food he eats
And pleased with what he gets,
Come hither, come hither, come hither:
   Here shall he see
   No enemy
But winter and rough weather.

SHAKESPEARE

"Blow, blow"

Blow, blow, thou winter wind,
Thou are not so unkind
   As man's ingratitude;
Thy tooth is not so keen
Because thou art not seen,
   Although thy breath be rude.
Heigh-ho! sing, heigh-ho! unto the green holly:
Most friendship is feigning, most loving mere folly:
   Then, heigh-ho! the holly!
   This life is most jolly.

Freeze, freeze, thou bitter sky,
Thou dost not bite so nigh
   As benefits forgot:
Though thou the waters warp,
Thy sting is not so sharp
   As friend remembered not.
Heigh-ho! sing, heigh-ho! unto the green holly:
Most friendship is feigning, most loving mere folly:
   Then, heigh-ho! the holly!
   This life is most jolly.

SHAKESPEARE

"It was a lover"

It was a lover and his lass,
   With a hey, and a ho, and a hey nonino!
That o'er the green corn-field did pass,
   In spring time, the only pretty ring time,
When birds do sing, hey ding a ding, ding;
   Sweet lovers love the spring.

Between the acres of the rye,
   With a hey, and a ho, and a hey nonino!
Those pretty country folks would lie,
   In spring time, the only pretty ring time,
When birds do sing, hey ding a ding, ding;
   Sweet lovers love the spring.

This carol they began that hour,
  With a hey, and a ho, and a hey nonino!
How that a life was but a flower
  In spring-time, the only pretty ring time,
When birds do sing, hey ding a ding, ding;
  Sweet lovers love the spring.

And therefore take the present time,
  With a hey, and a ho, and a hey nonino!
For love is crownèd with the prime
  In spring time, the only pretty ring time,
When birds do sing, hey ding a ding, ding;
  Sweet lovers love the spring.

SHAKESPEARE

"O mistress mine"

O mistress mine, where are you roaming?
O stay and hear; your true love's coming,
  That can sing both high and low.
Trip no further, pretty sweeting;
Journeys end in lovers' meeting,
  Every wise man's son doth know.

What is love? 'Tis not hereafter;
Present mirth hath present laughter;
  What's to come is still unsure.
In delay there lies no plenty;
Then come kiss me, sweet and twenty;
  Youth's a stuff will not endure.

SHAKESPEARE

"Come away, death"

Come away, come away, death,
  And in sad cypress let me be laid.
Fly away, fly away, breath;
  I am slain by a fair cruel maid.
My shroud of white, stuck all with yew,

O! prepare it.
My part of death, no one so true
    Did share it.

Not a flower, not a flower sweet,
    On my black coffin let there be strown;
Not a friend, not a friend greet
    My poor corpse, where my bones shall be thrown.
A thousand thousand sighs to save,
    Lay me, O! where
Sad true lover never find my grave,
    To weep there.

SHAKESPEARE

"Take, O! take"

Take, O! take those lips away,
    That so sweetly were forsworn,
And those eyes, the break of day,
    Lights that do mislead the morn;
But my kisses bring again,
                        bring again,
Seals of love, but sealed in vain,
                        sealed in vain.

SHAKESPEARE

"Full fathom five"

Full fathom five thy father lies;
    Of his bones are coral made;
Those are pearls, that were his eyes;
    Nothing of him that doth fade
But doth suffer a sea-change
Into something rich and strange.
Sea-nymphs hourly ring his knell.
                        Ding-dong!
Hark, now I hear them
    Ding dong, bell!

SHAKESPEARE

"Fear no more"

Fear no more the heat o' the sun
    Nor the furious winter's rages;
Thou thy worldly task hast done,
    Home art gone and ta'en thy wages.
Golden lads and girls all must,
As chimney-sweepers, come to dust.

Fear no more the frown o' the great,
    Thou art past the tyrant's stroke;
Care no more to clothe and eat;
    To thee the reed is as the oak.
The sceptre, learning, physic, must
All follow this, and come to dust.

Fear no more the lightning-flash,
    Nor the all-dreaded thunder-stone:
Fear not slander, censure rash;
    Thou hast finished joy and moan.
All lovers young, all lovers must
Consign to thee, and come to dust.

SHAKESPEARE

To His Love

Come away! come, sweet Love!
    The golden morning breaks;
All the earth, all the air,
    Of love and pleasure speaks.
Teach thine arms then to embrace,
    And sweet rosy lips to kiss,
    And mix our souls in mutual bliss:
Eyes were made for beauty's grace,
Viewing, rueing, love's long pain,
    Procured by beauty's rude disdain.

Come away! come, sweet Love!
    The golden morning wastes,

While the sun, from his sphere,
  His fiery arrows casts,
Making all the shadows fly,
    Playing, staying, in the grove
    To entertain the stealth of love.
Thither, sweet Love, let us hie,
    Flying, dying, in desire,
    Winged with sweet hopes and heavenly fire.

Come away! come, sweet Love!
    Do not in vain adorn
Beauty's grace, that should rise
    Like to the naked morn.
Lilies on the river's side,
    And fair Cyprian flowers new-blown,
    Desire no beauties but their own:
Ornament is nurse of pride.
    Pleasure measure love's delight:
    Haste then, sweet Love, our wishèd flight!

                                        ANON.

"Kind are her answers"

Kind are her answers,
But her performance keeps no day;
Breaks time, as dancers,
From their own music when they stray.
All her free favours and smooth words
Wing my hopes in vain.
O, did ever voice so sweet but only feign?
Can true love yield such delay,
Converting joy to pain?

Lost is our freedom
When we submit to women so:
Why do we need 'em
When, in their best, they work our woe?
There is no wisdom
Can alter ends by Fate prefixt.

O, why is the good of man with evil mixt?
Never were days yet called two
But one night went betwixt.

THOMAS CAMPION

"There is a garden"

There is a garden in her face
Where roses and white lilies grow;
A heavenly paradise is that place
Wherein all pleasant fruits do flow.
     There cherries grow which none may buy,
     Till "Cherry ripe" themselves do cry.

Those cherries fairly do enclose
Of orient pearl a double row,
Which when her lovely laughter shows,
They look like rose-buds filled with snow;
     Yet them nor peer nor prince can buy,
     Till "Cherry ripe" themselves do cry.

Her eyes like angels watch them still,
Her brows like bended bows do stand,
Threatening with piercing frowns to kill
All that attempt with eye or hand
     Those sacred cherries to come nigh
     Till "Cherry ripe" themselves do cry.

THOMAS CAMPION

"Follow thy fair sun"

Follow thy fair sun, unhappy shadow!
    Though thou be black as night,
    And she made all of light,
Yet follow thy fair sun, unhappy shadow!

Follow her, whose light thy light depriveth!
    Though here thou liv'st disgraced,
    And she in heaven is placed,
Yet follow her whose light the world reviveth!

Follow those pure beams, whose beauty burneth!
   That so have scorchèd thee
   As thou still black must be
Till her kind beams thy black to brightness turneth.

Follow her, while yet her glory shineth!
   There comes a luckless night
   That will dim all her light;
And this the black unhappy shade divineth.

Follow still, since so thy fates ordainèd!
   The sun must have his shade,
   Till both at once do fade,
The sun still proved, the shadow still disdainèd.

Thomas Campion

"Come, you pretty false-eyed wanton"

Come, you pretty false-eyed wanton,
   Leave your crafty smiling!
Think you to escape me now
   With slipp'ry words beguiling?
No; you mocked me th'other day;
   When you got loose, you fled away;
But, since I have caught you now,
   I'll clip your wings for flying:
Smoth'ring kisses fast I'll heap
   And keep you so from crying.

Sooner may you count the stars
   And number hail down-pouring,
Tell the osiers of the Thames,
   Or Goodwin sands devouring,
Than the thick-showered kisses here
   Which now thy tired lips must bear.
Such a harvest never was
   So rich and full of pleasure,
But 'tis spent as soon as reaped,
   So trustless is love's treasure.

Thomas Campion

osiers = willows

To His Mistress, the
Queen of Bohemia

You meaner beauties of the night,
  That poorly satisfy our eyes
More by your number than your light,
  You common people of the skies,
  What are you when the moon shall rise?

You curious chanters of the wood,
  That warble forth Dame Nature's lays,
Thinking your passions understood
  By your weak accents; what's your praise
  When Philomel her voice shall raise?

You violets that first appear,
  By your pure purple mantles known
Like the proud virgins of the year,
  As if the spring were all your own;
  What are you when the rose is blown?

So, when my mistress shall be seen
  In form and beauty of her mind,
By virtue first, then choice, a Queen,
  Tell me, if she were not design'd
  Th' eclipse and glory of her kind?

                            SIR HENRY WOTTON

"Love not me for comely grace"

Love not me for comely grace,
For my pleasing eye or face,
Nor for any outward part:
No, nor for a constant heart!
For these may fail or turn to ill:
        So thou and I shall sever.
Keep therefore a true woman's eye,
And love me still, but know not why!

So hast thou the same reason still
To doat upon me ever.

ANON. (from JOHN WILBYE,
Second Set of Madrigals)

"Since first I saw your face"

Since first I saw your face I resolved to honour and renown ye;
If now I be disdained I wish my heart had never known ye.
What? I that loved and you that liked shall we begin to wrangle?
No, no, no, my heart is fast, and cannot disentangle.

If I admire or praise you too much, that fault you may forgive me,
Or if my hands had strayed but a touch, then justly might you leave me.
I asked you leave, you bade me love; is't now a time to chide me?
No, no, no, I'll love you still what fortune e'er betide me.

The sun whose beams most glorious are, rejecteth no beholder,
And your sweet beauty past compare made my poor eyes the bolder:
Where beauty moves, and wit delights and signs of kindness bind me,
There, O there! where'er I go I'll leave my heart behind me.

ANON. (from THOMAS FORD,
Music of Sundry Kinds)

"Once did my thoughts"

Once did my thoughts both ebb and flow,
    As passion did them move;
Once did I hope, straight fear again,—
    And then I was in love.

Once did I waking spend the night,
    And tell how minutes move.
Once did I wishing waste the day,—
    And then I was in love.

Once, by my carving true love's knot,
    The weeping trees did prove

That wounds and tears were both our lot,—
   And then I was in love.

Once did I breathe another's breath
   And in my mistress move,
Once was I not mine own at all,—
   And then I was in love.

Once wore I bracelets made of hair,
   And collars did approve,
Once wore my clothes made out of wax,—
   And then I was in love.

Once did I sonnet to my saint,
   My soul in numbers move,
Once did I tell a thousand lies,—
   And then I was in love.

Once in my ear did dangling hang
   A little turtle-dove,
Once, in a word, I was a fool,—
   And then I was in love.

ANON. (from ROBERT JONES,
The Muses' Garden of Delight)

"Golden slumbers"

Golden slumbers kiss your eyes,
Smiles awake you when you rise.
Sleep, pretty wantons, do not cry,
And I will sing a lullaby:
Rock them, rock them, lullaby.

Care is heavy, therefore sleep you;
You are care, and care must keep you.
Sleep, pretty wantons, do not cry,
And I will sing a lullaby:
Rock them, rock them, lullaby.

THOMAS DEKKER

"Oh, no more, no more!"

Oh, no more, no more! too late
   Sighs are spent; the burning tapers
Of a life as chaste as fate,
   Pure as are unwritten papers,
Are burnt out: no heat, no light
Now remains; 'tis ever night.
    Love is dead; let lovers' eyes,
      Locked in endless dreams,
      The extremes of all extremes,
    Ope no more, for now Love dies.
Now Love dies,—implying
Love's martyrs must be ever, ever dying.

JOHN FORD

To Daffodils

Fair daffodils, we weep to see
   You haste away so soon:
As yet the early-rising sun
   Has not attain'd his noon.
     Stay, stay,
    Until the hasting day
      Has run
    But to the Evensong;
And, having pray'd together, we
    Will go with you along.

We have short time to stay, as you,
   We have as short a spring;
As quick a growth to meet decay,
   As you, or any thing.
     We die,
As your hours do, and dry
     Away,
    Like to the summer's rain;
Or as the pearls of morning's dew
    Ne'er to be found again.

ROBERT HERRICK

To the Virgins
to Make Much of Time

Gather ye rosebuds while ye may,
   Old time is still a-flying:
And this same flower that smiles today,
   Tomorrow will be dying.

The glorious lamp of heaven, the sun,
   The higher he's a-getting;
The sooner will his race be run,
   And nearer he's to setting.

That age is best, which is the first,
   When youth and blood are warmer;
But being spent, the worse, and worst
   Times, still succeed the former.

Then be not coy, but use your time;
   And while ye may, go marry:
For having lost but once your prime,
   You may for ever tarry.

                ROBERT HERRICK

"Cherry-ripe"

Cherry-ripe, ripe, ripe, I cry,
Full and fair ones; come and buy:
If so be, you ask me where
They do grow? I answer, there,
Where my Julia's lips do smile;
There's the land, or cherry-isle:
Whose plantations fully show
All the year, where cherries grow.

                ROBERT HERRICK

"Dew sat on Julia's hair"

Dew sat on Julia's hair,
   And spangled too,
Like leaves that laden are

With trembling Dew:
Or glitter'd to my sight,
   As when the beams
Have their reflected light
   Danc'd by the streams.

ROBERT HERRICK

The Night Piece, to Julia

Her eyes the glow-worm lend thee,
The shooting stars attend thee;
   And the elves also,
   Whose little eyes glow,
Like the sparks of fire, befriend thee.

No will-o'-the-wisp mislight thee;
Nor snake, or slow-worm bite thee:
   But on, on thy way
   Not making a stay,
Since ghost there's none to affright thee.

Let not the dark thee cumber;
What though the moon does slumber?
   The stars of the night
   Will lend thee their light,
Like tapers clear without number.

Then Julia let me woo thee,
Thus, thus to come unto me:
   And when I shall meet
   Thy silv'ry feet,
My soul I'll pour into thee.

ROBERT HERRICK

To Daisies,
Not to Shut So Soon

Shut not so soon; the dull-ey'd night
   Has not as yet begun
To make a seizure on the light,
   Or to seal up the sun.

No marigolds yet closèd are;
    No shadows great appear;
Nor doth the early shepherds' star
    Shine like a spangle here.

Stay but till my Julia close
    Her life-begetting eye;
And let the whole world then dispose
    Itself to live or die.

             ROBERT HERRICK

"So look the mornings"

So look the mornings when the sun
Paints them with fresh vermillion:
So cherries blush, and kathern pears,
And apricocks, in youthful years:
So corals look more lovely red,
And rubies lately polishèd:
So purest diaper doth shine,
Stain'd by the beams of claret wine:
As Julia looks when she doth dress
Her either cheek with bashfulness.

             ROBERT HERRICK

kathern = katherine: *diaper* = linen

"Fain would I change that note"

Fain would I change that note
To which fond love hath charm'd me,
Long long to sing by rote,
Fancying that that harm'd me:
Yet when this thought doth come,
"Love is the perfect sum
Of all delight,"
I have no other choice
Either for pen or voice
To sing or write.

O Love, they wrong thee much
That say thy sweet is bitter,
When thy rich fruit is such
As nothing can be sweeter.
Fair house of joy and bliss,
Where truest pleasure is,
I do adore thee;
I know thee what thou art,
I serve thee with my heart,
And fall before thee.

> Anon. (from T. Hume,
> *Musical Humours*)

Song

Go, lovely Rose!
  Tell her that wastes her time and me,
That now she knows,
    When I resemble her to thee,
    How sweet and fair she seems to be.

Tell her that's young,
  And shuns to have her graces spied,
That hadst thou sprung
    In deserts, where no men abide,
    Thou must have uncommended died.

Small is the worth
  Of beauty from the light retired;
Bid her come forth,
    Suffer herself to be desired,
    And not blush so to be admired.

Then die! That she
  The common fate of all things rare
May read in thee:
    How small a part of time they share,
    That are so wondrous sweet and fair!

> Edmund Waller

The Silver Swan

The silver swan, who living had no note,
When death approached, unlocked her silent throat,
Leaning her breast against the reedy shore,
Thus sung her first and last, and sung no more:
Farewell all joys! O death, come close mine eyes;
More geese than swans now live, more fools than wise.

ANON. (from O. GIBBONS,
Madrigals & Motets)

"Weep you no more"

Weep you no more, sad fountains;
    What need you flow so fast?
Look how the snowy mountains
    Heaven's sun doth gently waste!
But my sun's heavenly eyes
    View not your weeping,
    That now lies sleeping
Softly, now softly lies
            Sleeping.

Sleep is a reconciling,
    A rest that peace begets;
Doth not the sun rise smiling
    When fair at ev'n he sets?
Rest you then, rest, sad eyes!
    Melt not in weeping,
    While she lies sleeping,
Softly, now softly lies
            Sleeping.

ANON. (from J. Dowland,
Songs or Airs)

"I saw my Lady weep"

I saw my Lady weep,
And Sorrow proud to be advancèd so
In those fair eyes where all perfections keep.

Her face was full of woe,
But such a woe (believe me) as wins more hearts
Than Mirth can do with her enticing parts.

Sorrow was there made fair,
And Passion wise; tears a delightful thing;
Silence beyond all speech a wisdom rare;
    She made her sighs to sing,
And all things with so sweet a sadness move
As made my heart at once both grieve and love.

O fairer than aught else
The world can show! leave off in time to grieve.
Enough, enough: your joyful look excels:
    Tears kill the heart, believe.
O strive not to be excellent in woe,
Which only breeds your beauty's overthrow.

ANON. (from J. Dowland,
Songs or Airs)

"Slow, slow, fresh fount"

Slow, slow, fresh fount, keep time with my salt tears:
    Yet slower, yet; oh, faintly, gentle springs,
List to the heavy part the music bears,
    Woe weeps out her division when she sings.
        Droop herbs and flowers;
        Fall grief in showers,
        Our beauties are not ours;
            Oh, I could still,
Like melting snow upon some craggy hill,
        Drop, drop, drop, drop,
Since nature's pride is now a withered daffodil.

BEN JONSON

Song, to Celia

Drink to me only with thine eyes,
    And I will pledge with mine;
Or leave a kiss but in the cup,

And I'll not look for wine.
The thirst that from the soul doth rise
    Doth ask a drink divine:
But might I of Jove's nectar sup,
    I would not change for thine.

I sent thee late a rosy wreath,
    Not so much honouring thee,
As giving it a hope that there
    It could not withered be.
But thou thereon didst only breathe,
    And sent'st it back to me:
Since when it grows, and smells, I swear,
    Not of itself, but thee.

BEN JONSON

The Triumph of Charis

See the chariot at hand here of Love,
    Wherein my lady rideth!
Each that draws is a swan or a dove,
    And well the car Love guideth.
As she goes, all hearts do duty
    Unto her beauty;
And enamoured do wish, so they might
    But enjoy such a sight,
That they still were to run by her side,
Through swords, through seas, whither she would ride.

Do but look on her eyes, they do light
    All that Love's world compriseth!
Do but look on her hair, it is bright
    As Love's star when it riseth!
Do but mark, her forehead's smoother
    Than words that soothe her;
And from her arched brows such a grace
    Sheds itself through the face,
As alone there triumphs to the life
All the gain, all the good of the elements' strife.

Have you seen but a bright lily grow
    Before rude hands have touched it?
Have you marked but the fall of the snow
    Before the soil hath smutched it?
Have you felt the wool o' the beaver,
      Or swan's down ever?
Or have smelt o' the bud o' the brier,
      Or the nard i' the fire?
Or have tasted the bag o' the bee?
Oh so white, oh so soft, oh so sweet is she!

                        BEN JONSON

nard = an aromatic ointment

"Come, Sleep"

Come, Sleep, and with thy sweet deceiving
    Lock me in delight awhile!
    Let some passing dreams beguile
    All my fancies; that from thence
    I may feel an influence,
All my powers of care bereaving!

Though but a shadow, but a sliding,
    Let me know some little joy!
    We that suffer long annoy
    Are contented with a thought
    Through an idle fancy wrought:
Oh, let my joys have some abiding!

                FRANCIS BEAUMONT and
                   JOHN FLETCHER

"Care-charming Sleep"

Care-charming Sleep, thou easer of all woes,
Brother to Death, sweetly thyself dispose
On this afflicted prince; fall like a cloud,
In gentle showers; give nothing that is loud,
Or painful to his slumbers; easy, light,

And as a purling stream, thou son of Night
Pass by his troubled senses; sing his pain,
Like hollow murmuring wind or silver rain;
Into this prince gently, oh, gently slide,
And kiss him into slumbers like a bride.

JOHN FLETCHER

"Come hither, you that love"

Come hither, you that love, and hear me sing
    Of joys still growing,
Green, fresh, and lusty as the pride of spring,
    And ever blowing.
Come hither, youths that blush, and dare not know
    What is desire;
And old men, worse than you, that cannot blow
    One spark of fire;
And with the power of my enchanting song,
Boys shall be able men, and old men young.

Come hither, you that hope, and you that cry;
    Leave off complaining;
Youth, strength, and beauty, that shall never die,
    Are here remaining.
Come hither, fools, and blush you stay so long
    From being blessed;
And mad men, worse than you, that suffer wrong,
    Yet seek no rest;
And in an hour, with my enchanting song,
You shall be ever pleased, and young maids long.

JOHN FLETCHER

"Hear, ye ladies"

Hear, ye ladies that despise,
    What the mighty Love has done;
Fear examples, and be wise:
    Fair Calisto was a nun;

Leda, sailing on the stream
  To deceive the hopes of man,
Love accounting but a dream,
  Doted on a silver swan;
    Danaë, in a brazen tower,
    Where no love was, loved a shower.

Hear, ye ladies that are coy,
  What the mighty Love can do;
Fear the fierceness of the boy:
  The chaste moon he makes to woo;
Vesta, kindling holy fires,
  Circled round about with spies.
Never dreaming loose desires,
  Doting at the altar dies;
    Ilion, in a short hour, higher
    He can build, and once more fire.

JOHN FLETCHER

"Now the lusty spring"

Now the lusty spring is seen;
  Golden yellow, gaudy blue,
  Daintily invite the view.
Everywhere on every green,
Roses blushing as they blow,
  And enticing men to pull,
Lilies whiter than the snow,
  Woodbines of sweet honey full:
    All love's emblems, and all cry,
    "Ladies, if not plucked, we die."

Yet the lusty spring hath stayed;
  Blushing red and purest white
  Daintily to love invite
Every woman, every maid.
Cherries kissing as they grow,
  And inviting men to taste,
Apples even ripe below,

Winding gently to the waist:
All love's emblems, and all cry.
"Ladies, if not plucked, we die."

JOHN FLETCHER

"*Why so pale and wan*"

Why so pale and wan, fond lover?
    Prithee why so pale?
Will, when looking well can't move her,
    Looking ill prevail?
    Prithee why so pale?

Why so dull and mute, young sinner?
    Prithee why so mute?
Will, when speaking well can't win her,
    Saying nothing do 't?
    Prithee why so mute?

Quit, quit, for shame; this will not move,
    This cannot take her;
If of herself she will not love,
    Nothing can make her:
    The devil take her!

SIR JOHN SUCKLING

"*Let her give her hand*"

Let her give her hand, her glove;
Let her sigh and swear she dies;
He that thinks he hath her love,
I shall never think him wise:
    For be the old love ne'er so true,
    She is ever for the new.

One nail drives another forth;
Land must lose where sea doth win;
Last that comes, though least of worth,

Drives him out that first was in:
  So be the old love ne'er so true,
  She is ever for the new.

Store of dishes makes the feast;
Shift of clothes is sweet and clean;
Change of pasture fats the beast,
Think you then she will be lean?
  For be the old love ne'er so true,
  She is ever for the new.

                                        ANON.

"So, so"

        So, so,
Lo, lilies fade, before the roses show
Themselves in Bow-dye, summer's livery,
    Feasting the curious eye
    With choice variety;
        While as before
        We did adore
            Narcissus in his prime,
    Now roses do delight
    The nicer appetite:
Such is the vast disparity of time.

        So, so,
One woman fades, before another know
What 'tis to be in love: but in a trice
    All men do sacrifice
    To the latter, and despise
        Her whom before
        They did adore
            Like lilies in their prime;
    Since now her sparkling eyes
    Are darkened in disguise:
Such is the sad disparity of time.

                            WILLIAM CLERKE

Bow-dye = a scarlet dye made at Bow.

"There is a lady . . ."

There is a lady sweet and kind,
Was never face so pleased my mind;
I did but see her passing by,
And yet I love her till I die.

Her gesture, motion, and her smiles,
Her wit, her voice, my heart beguiles,
Beguiles my heart, I know not why,
And yet I love her till I die.

Her free behaviour, winning looks,
Will make a lawyer burn his books;
I touched her not, alas! not I,
And yet I love her till I die.

Had I her fast betwixt mine arms,
Judge you that think such sports were harms,
Were't any harm? no, no, fie, fie,
For I will love her till I die.

Should I remain confinèd there
So long as Phoebus in his sphere,
I to request, she to deny,
Yet would I love her till I die.

Cupid is wingèd and doth range,
Her country so my love doth change:
But change she earth, or change she sky,
Yet will I love her till I die.

ANON.

"Wake all the dead!"

Wake all the dead! what ho! what ho!
How soundly they sleep whose pillows lie low!
They mind not poor lovers who walk above
On the decks of the world in storms of love.
    No whisper now nor glance can pass

Through wickets or through panes of glass;
For our windows and doors are shut and barred.
Lie close in the church, and in the churchyard;
In every grave make room, make room!
The world's at an end, and we come, we come.

The state is now Love's foe, Love's foe;
Has seized on his arms, his quiver and bow;
Has pinioned his wings, and fettered his feet,
Because he made way for lovers to meet.
But, O sad chance, his judge was old;
Hearts cruel grow when blood grows cold.
No man being young his process would draw.
O heavens, that love should be subject to law!
Lovers go woo the dead, the dead!
Lie two in a grave, and to bed, to bed!

SIR WILLIAM DAVENANT

"Farewell, ungrateful traitor"

Farewell, ungrateful traitor,
    Farewell, my perjur'd swain;
Let never injur'd creature
    Believe a man again.
The pleasure of possessing
Surpasses all expressing,
But 'tis too short a blessing,
    And love too long a pain.

'Tis easy to deceive us
    In pity of your pain,
But when we love you leave us
    To rail at you in vain.
Before we have descried it,
There is no bliss beside it,
But she that once has tried it
    Will never love again.

The passion you pretended
    Was only to obtain;

But when the charm is ended
    The charmer you disdain.
Your love by ours we measure,
Till we have lost our treasure;
But dying is a pleasure
    When living is a pain.

JOHN DRYDEN

"After the pangs"

After the pangs of a desperate lover,
When day and night I have sigh'd all in vain,
Ah what a pleasure it is to discover
In her eyes pity, who causes my pain!

When with unkindness our love at a stand is,
And both have punish'd ourselves with the pain,
Ah what a pleasure the touch of her hand is!
Ah what a pleasure to press it again!

When the denial comes fainter and fainter,
And her eyes give what her tongue does deny,
Ah what a trembling I feel when I venture!
Ah what a trembling does usher my joy!

When, with a sigh, she accords me the blessing,
And her eyes twinkle 'twixt pleasure and pain,
Ah what a joy 'tis, beyond all expressing!
Ah what a joy to hear, Shall we again?

JOHN DRYDEN

Song for a Girl

Young I am, and yet unskill'd
How to make a lover yield;
How to keep, or how to gain,
When to love, and when to feign.

Take me, take me, some of you,
While I yet am young and true;
Ere I can my soul disguise,
Heave my breasts, and roll my eyes.

Stay not till I learn the way,
How to lie, and to betray:
He that has me first, is blest,
For I may deceive the rest.

Could I find a blooming youth,
Full of love, and full of truth,
Brisk, and of a jaunty mien,
I should long to be fifteen.

JOHN DRYDEN

"All, all of a piece"

All, all of a piece throughout;
Thy chase had a beast in view,
Thy wars brought nothing about,
Thy lovers were all untrue;
'Tis well an old age is out
And time to begin a new.

JOHN DRYDEN

Love and Life

All my past life is mine no more,
    The flying hours are gone:
Like transitory dreams giv'n o'er,
Whose images are kept in store
    By memory alone.

The time that is to come is not,
    How can it then be mine?
The present moment's all my lot,

And that, as fast as it is got,
  Phillis, is only thine.

Then talk not of inconstancy,
  False hearts and broken vows;
If I, by miracle, can be
This live-long minute true to thee,
  'Tis all that heav'n allows.

JOHN WILMOT,
EARL OF ROCHESTER

A Song

Absent from thee I languish still,
  Then ask me not, when I return?
The straying fool 'twill plainly kill,
  To wish all day, all night to mourn.

Dear; from thine arms then let me fly,
  That my fantastic mind may prove
The torments it deserves to try,
  That tears my fixt heart from my love.

When wearied with a world of woe
  To thy safe bosom I retire,
Where love, and peace, and truth does flow,
  May I contented there expire.

Lest once more wand'ring from that heav'n,
  I fall on some base heart unblest;
Faithless to thee, false, unforgiv'n,
  And lose my everlasting rest.

JOHN WILMOT,
EARL OF ROCHESTER

"Love in her eyes"

Love in her eyes sits playing,
  And sheds delicious death;
Love in her lips is straying,

And warbling in her breath;
Love on her breast sits panting,
And swells with soft desire;
Nor grace, nor charm, is wanting
To set the heart on fire.

JOHN GAY

"O ruddier than the cherry"

O ruddier than the cherry,
O sweeter than the berry,
O nymph more bright
Than moonshine night,
Like kidlings blithe and merry.
Ripe as the melting cluster,
No lily has such lustre,
Yet hard to tame,
As raging flame,
And fierce as storms that bluster.

JOHN GAY

"If the heart of a man"

If the heart of a man is depressed with cares,
The mist is dispelled when a woman appears;
Like the notes of a fiddle, she sweetly, sweetly,
Raises the spirits, and charms our ears.
Roses and lilies her cheeks disclose,
But her ripe lips are more sweet than those.
Press her,
Caress her,
With blisses,
Her kisses
Dissolve us in pleasure and soft repose.

JOHN GAY

"Here's to the maiden"

Here's to the maiden of bashful fifteen;
  Here's to the widow of fifty;
Here's to the flaunting extravagant quean,
  And here's to the housewife that's thrifty.

Chorus

  Let the toast pass, —
  Drink to the lass,
I'll warrant she'll prove an excuse for the glass.

Here's to the charmer whose dimples we prize;
  Now to the maid who has none, sir:
Here's to the girl with a pair of blue eyes,
  And here's to the nymph with but *one*, sir.
    Chorus. Let the toast pass, &c.

Here's to the maid with a bosom of snow;
  Now to her that's as brown as a berry:
Here's to the wife with a face full of woe,
  And now to the girl that is merry.
    Chorus. Let the toast pass, &c.

For let 'em be clumsy, or let 'em be slim,
  Young or ancient, I care not a feather;
So fill a pint bumper quite up to the brim,
  And let us e'en toast them together.
    Chorus. Let the toast pass, &c.

                    RICHARD BRINSLEY SHERIDAN

The Three Pigeons

Let schoolmasters puzzle their brain,
  With grammar, and nonsense, and learning;
Good liquor, I stoutly maintain,
  Gives genius a better discerning.
Let them brag of their heathenish gods,
  Their Lethes, their Styxes, and Stygians,

Their Quis and their Quaes and their Quods,
   They're all but a parcel of pigeons.
        Toroddle, toroddle, toroll.

When Methodist preachers come down,
   A-preaching that drinking is sinful,
I'll wager the rascals a crown,
   They always preach best with a skinful.
But when you come down with your pence,
   For a slice of their scurvy religion,
I'll leave it to all men of sense,
   But you, my good friend, are the pigeon.
        Toroddle, toroddle, toroll.

Then come, put the jorum about,
   And let us be merry and clever,
Our hearts and our liquors are stout,
   Here's the Three Jolly Pigeons for ever!
Let some cry up woodcock or hare,
   Your bustards, your ducks, and your widgeons;
But of all the gay birds in the air,
   Here's a health to the Three Jolly Pigeons!
        Toroddle, toroddle, toroll.

OLIVER GOLDSMITH

"My silks and fine array"

My silks and fine array,
My smiles and languish'd air,
By Love are driv'n away;
And mournful lean Despair
Brings me yew to deck my grave:
Such end true lovers have.

His face is fair as heav'n
When springing buds unfold;
O why to him was 't giv'n
Whose heart is wintry cold?
His breast is Love's all-worship'd tomb,
Where all Love's pilgrims come.

Bring me an axe and spade,
Bring me a winding-sheet;
When I my grave have made
Let winds and tempests beat:
Then down I'll lie as cold as clay.
True love doth pass away!

WILLIAM BLAKE

"*Ae fond kiss*"

Ae fond kiss, and then we sever;
Ae farewell and then for ever!
Deep in heart-wrung tears I'll pledge thee,
Warring sighs and groans I'll wage thee.
Who shall say that fortune grieves him
While the star of hope she leaves him?
Me, nae chearfu' twinkle lights me;
Dark despair around benights me.

I'll ne'er blame my partial fancy,
Næthing could resist my Nancy:
But to see her, was to love her;
Love but her, and love for ever.
Had we never lov'd sæ kindly,
Had we never lov'd sæ blindly,
Never met—or never parted,
We had ne'er been broken-hearted.

Fare thee weel, thou first and fairest!
Fare thee weel, thou best and dearest!
Thine be ilka joy and treasure,
Peace, Enjoyment, Love and Pleasure!
Ae fond kiss, and then we sever;
Ae fareweel, alas! for ever!
Deep in heart-wrung tears I'll pledge thee,
Warring sighs and groans I'll wage thee.

ROBERT BURNS

"Ye banks and braes"

Ye banks and bræs o' bonie Doon,
　　How can ye bloom sæ fresh and fair;
How can ye chant, ye little birds,
　　And I sæ weary fu' o' care!
Thou'll break my heart thou warbling bird,
　　That wantons thro' the flowering thorn:
Thou minds me o' departed joys,
　　Departed never to return.

Oft hæ I rov'd by bonie Doon,
　　To see the rose and woodbine twine;
And ilka bird sang o' its luve,
　　And fondly sæ did I o' mine.
Wi' lightsome heart I pu'd a rose,
　　Fu' sweet upon its thorny tree;
And my fause luver staw my rose,
　　But, ah! he left the thorn wi' me.

ROBERT BURNS

staw = stole

"O my Luve's like a red, red rose"

O my Luve's like a red, red rose,
　　That's newly sprung in June.
O my Luve's like the melodie
　　That's sweetly play'd in tune.

As fair art thou, my bonie lass,
　　So deep in luve am I;
And I will love thee still, my Dear,
　　Till a' the seas gang dry.

Till a' the seas gang dry, my Dear,
　　And the rocks melt wi' the sun:
I will love thee still, my Dear,
　　While the sands o' life shall run.

And fare thee weel, my only Luve!
  And fare thee weel, a while!
And I will come again, my Luve,
  Tho' it were ten thousand mile!

ROBERT BURNS

"Oh wert thou in the cauld blast"

Oh wert thou in the cauld blast,
  On yonder lea, on yonder lea;
My plaidie to the angry airt,
  I'd shelter thee, I'd shelter thee:
Or did misfortune's bitter storms
  Around thee blaw, around thee blaw,
Thy bield should be my bosom,
  To share it a', to share it a'.

Or were I in the wildest waste,
  Sæ black and bare, sæ black and bare,
The desart were a paradise,
  If thou wert there, if thou wert there.
Or were I monarch o' the globe,
  Wi' thee to reign, wi' thee to reign;
The brightest jewel in my crown,
  Wad be my queen, wad be my queen.

ROBERT BURNS

airt = quarter (of the wind): *bield* = shelter

Echo

How sweet the answer Echo makes
    To Music at night,
When, rous'd by lute or horn, she wakes,
And, far away, o'er lawns and lakes,
    Goes answering light!

Yet Love hath echoes truer far,
    And far more sweet,

Than e'er beneath the moonlight's star,
Of horn, or lute, or soft guitar,
The songs repeat.

'Tis when the sigh, in youth sincere,
And only then, —
The sigh that's breath'd for one to hear,
Is by that one, that only dear,
Breath'd back again.

THOMAS MOORE

"Believe me, if all those endearing young charms"

Believe me, if all those endearing young charms,
Which I gaze on so fondly today,
Were to change by tomorrow, and fleet in my arms,
Like fairy-gifts fading away,
Thou wouldst still be ador'd, as this moment thou art,
Let thy loveliness fade as it will,
And around the dear ruin each wish of my heart
Would entwine itself verdantly still.

It is not while beauty and youth are thine own,
And thy cheeks unprofan'd by a tear,
That the fervour and faith of a soul can be known,
To which time will but make thee more dear;
No, the heart that has truly lov'd never forgets,
But as truly loves on to the close,
As the sun-flower turns on her god, when he sets,
The same look which she turn'd when he rose.

THOMAS MOORE

"This life is all chequer'd with pleasures and woes"

This life is all chequer'd with pleasures and woes,
That chase one another like waves of the deep,—
Each brightly or darkly, as onward it flows,

Reflecting our eyes, as they sparkle or weep.
So closely our whims on our miseries tread,
    That the laugh is awak'd ere the tear can be dried;
And, as fast as the rain-drop of Pity is shed,
    The goose-plumage of Folly can turn it aside.
But pledge me the cup—if existence should cloy,
    With hearts ever happy, and heads ever wise,
Be ours the light Sorrow, half-sister to Joy,
    And the light brilliant Folly that flashes and dies.

When Hylas was sent with his urn to the fount,
    Thro' fields full of light, with heart full of play,
Light rambled the boy, over meadow and mount,
    And neglected his task for the flowers on the way.
Thus many, like me, who in youth should have tasted
    The fountain that runs by Philosophy's shrine,
Their time with the flowers on the margin have wasted,
    And left their light urns all as empty as mine.
But pledge me the goblet—while Idleness weaves
    These flowerets together, should Wisdom but see
One bright drop or two that has fall'n on the leaves
    From her fountain divine, 'tis sufficient for me.

THOMAS MOORE

"The young May moon"

The young May moon is beaming, love,
The glow-worm's lamp is gleaming, love,
        How sweet to rove
        Through Morna's grove,
When the drowsy world is dreaming, love!
Then awake!—the heavens look bright, my dear,
'Tis never too late for delight, my dear,
        And the best of all ways
        To lengthen our days
Is to steal a few hours from the night, my dear.

Now all the world is sleeping, love,
But the Sage, his star-watch keeping, love,

And I, whose star,
        More glorious far,
Is the eye from that casement peeping, love.
Then awake!—till rise of sun, my dear,
The Sage's glass we'll shun, my dear,
        Or, in watching the flight
        Of bodies of light,
He might happen to take thee for one, my dear.

THOMAS MOORE

" 'Tis the last rose of summer"

'Tis the last rose of summer
    Left blooming alone;
All her lovely companions
    Are faded and gone;
No flower of her kindred,
    No rose-bud is nigh,
To reflect back her blushes,
    Or give sigh for sigh.

I'll not leave thee, thou lone one,
    To pine on the stem;
Since the lovely are sleeping,
    Go, sleep thou with them.
Thus kindly I scatter
    Thy leaves o'er the bed,
Where thy mates of the garden
    Lie scentless and dead.

So soon may *I* follow,
    When friendships decay,
And from Love's shining circle
    The gems drop away!
When true hearts lie wither'd,
    And fond ones are flown,
Oh! who would inhabit
    This bleak world alone?

THOMAS MOORE

"So, we'll go no more a roving"

So, we'll go no more a roving
   So late into the night,
Though the heart be still as loving,
   And the moon be still as bright.

For the sword outwears its sheath,
   And the soul wears out the breast,
And the heart must pause to breathe,
   And love itself have rest.

Though the night was made for loving,
   And the day returns too soon,
Yet we'll go no more a roving
   By the light of the moon.

GEORGE GORDON,
LORD BYRON

"Peggy said good morning"

Peggy said good morning and I said goodbye,
When farmers dib the corn and laddies sow the rye.
Young Peggy's face was commonsense and I was rather shy
When I met her in the morning when the farmers sow the rye.

Her half-laced boots fit tightly as she tripped along the grass,
And she set her foot so lightly where the early bee doth pass.
Oh, Peggy was a young thing, her face was commonsense,
I courted her about the spring and loved her ever thence.

Oh, Peggy was a young thing and bonny as to size;
Her lips were cherries of the spring and hazel were her eyes.
Oh, Peggy she was straight and tall as is the poplar-tree,
Smooth as the freestone of the wall, and very dear to me.

Oh, Peggy's gown was chocolate and full of cherries white;
I keep a bit on't for her sake and love her day and night.

I drest myself just like a prince and Peggy went to woo,
But she's been gone some ten years since, and I know not what to do.

JOHN CLARE

dib = to plant or sow with a dibble.

"Come hither, my dear one"

Come hither, my dear one, my choice one, and rare one,
   And let us be walking the meadows so fair,
Where on pilewort and daisies the eye fondly gazes,
   And the wind plays so sweet in thy bonny brown hair.

Come with thy maiden eye, lay silks and satins by;
   Come in thy russet or grey cotton gown;
Come to the meads, dear, where flags, sedge, and reeds appear,
   Rustling to soft winds and bowing low down.

Come with thy parted hair, bright eyes, and forehead bare;
   Come to the whitethorn that grows in the lane;
To banks of primroses, where sweetness reposes,
   Come, love, and let us be happy again.

Come where the violet flowers, come where the morning showers
   Pearl on the primrose and speedwell so blue;
Come to that clearest brook that ever runs round the nook
   Where you and I pledged our first love so true.

JOHN CLARE

"It was not in the winter"

It was not in the winter
   Our loving lot was cast!
It was the time of roses,
   We plucked them as we passed!

That churlish season never frowned
   On early lovers yet!

Oh no—the world was newly crowned
With flowers, when first we met.

'Twas twilight, and I bade you go,
   But still you held me fast;
It was the time of roses—
   We plucked them as we passed!

What else could peer my glowing cheek
   That tears began to stud?
And when I asked the like of Love
   You snatched a damask bud,

And oped it to the dainty core
   Still glowing to the last:
It was the time of roses,
   We plucked them as we passed!

THOMAS HOOD

peer = match

"How many times?"

How many times do I love thee, dear?
   Tell me how many thoughts there be
      In the atmosphere
      Of a new-fall'n year,
Whose white and sable hours appear
   The latest flake of Eternity:
So many times do I love thee, dear.

How many times do I love again?
   Tell me how many beads there are
      In a silver chain
      Of evening rain,
Unravelled from the tumbling main,
   And threading the eye of a yellow star:
So many times do I love again.

THOMAS LOVELL BEDDOES

"Now sleeps the crimson petal"

Now sleeps the crimson petal, now the white;
Nor waves the cypress in the palace walk;
Nor winks the gold fin in the porphyry font;
The fire-fly wakens; waken thou with me.

Now droops the milkwhite peacock like a ghost,
And like a ghost she glimmers on to me.

Now lies the Earth all Danaë to the stars,
And all thy heart lies open unto me.

Now slides the silent meteor on, and leaves
A shining furrow, as thy thoughts in me.

Now folds the lily all her sweetness up,
And slips into the bosom of the lake;
So fold thyself, my dearest, thou, and slip
Into my bosom and be lost in me.

ALFRED, LORD TENNYSON

"As I sat at the café"

As I sat at the café, I said to myself,
They may talk as they please about what they call pelf,
They may sneer as they like about eating and drinking,
But help it I cannot, I cannot help thinking
    How pleasant it is to have money, heigh ho!
    How pleasant it is to have money.

I sit at my table *en grand seigneur,*
And when I have done, throw a crust to the poor;
Not only the pleasure, one's self, of good living,
But also the pleasure of now and then giving.
    So pleasant it is to have money, heigh ho!
    So pleasant it is to have money.

It was but last winter I came up to Town,
But already I'm getting a little renown;

I make new acquaintance where'er I appear;
I am not too shy, and have nothing to fear.
   So pleasant it is to have money, heigh ho!
   So pleasant it is to have money.

I drive through the streets, and I care not a d-mn;
The people they stare, and they ask who I am;
And if I should chance to run over a cad,
I can pay for the damage if ever so bad.
   So pleasant it is to have money, heigh ho!
   So pleasant it is to have money.

We stroll to our box and look down on the pit,
And if it weren't low should be tempted to spit;
We loll and we talk until people look up,
And when it's half over we go out and sup.
   So pleasant it is to have money, heigh ho!
   So pleasant it is to have money.

The best of the tables and best of the fare—
And as for the others, the devil may care;
It isn't our fault if they dare not afford
To sup like a prince and be drunk as a lord.
   So pleasant it is to have money, heigh ho!
   So pleasant it is to have money.

We sit at our table and tipple champagne;
Ere one bottle goes, comes another again;
The waiters they skip and they scuttle about,
And the landlord attends us so civilly out.
   So pleasant it is to have money, heigh ho!
   So pleasant it is to have money.

It was but last winter I came up to Town,
But already I'm getting a little renown;
I get to good houses without much ado,
Am beginning to see the nobility too.
   So pleasant it is to have money, heigh ho!
   So pleasant it is to have money.

Oh dear! what a pity they ever should lose it!
For they are the gentry that know how to use it;

So grand and so graceful, such manners, such dinners,
But yet, after all, it is we are the winners.
   So pleasant it is to have money, heigh ho!
   So pleasant it is to have money.

Thus I sat at my table *en grand seigneur,*
And when I had done threw a crust to the poor;
Not only the pleasure, one's self, of good eating,
But also the pleasure of now and then treating.
   So pleasant it is to have money, heigh ho!
   So pleasant it is to have money.

They may talk as they please about what they call pelf,
And how one ought never to think of one's self,
And how pleasures of thought surpass eating and drinking—
My pleasure of thought is the pleasure of thinking
   How pleasant it is to have money, heigh ho!
   How pleasant it is to have money.

A. H. CLOUGH

pelf = money

Eton Boating Song

Jolly boating weather
   And a hay harvest breeze,
Blade on the feather,
   Shade off the trees,
Swing, swing, together,
   With your bodies between your knees.

Chorus

Swing, swing together
   With your bodies between your knees.

Skirting past the rushes,
   Ruffling o'er the weeds
Where the lock stream gushes
   Where the cygnet feeds.

Let us see how the wine-glass flushes
  At supper on Boveney meads.

Chorus

Harrow may be more clever,
  Rugby may make more row,
But we'll row, row for ever,
  Steady from stroke to bow,
And nothing in life shall sever
  The chain that is round us now.

Chorus

Others will fill our places,
  Dressed in the old light blue;
We'll recollect our races,
  We'll to the flag be true,
And youth will be still in our faces,
  When we cheer for an Eton crew.

Chorus

Twenty years hence this weather
  Will tempt us from office stools.
We may be slow on the feather,
  And seem to the boys old fools,
But we'll still swing together,
  And swear by the best of schools.

Chorus

WILLIAM CORY

"When I am dead"

When I am dead, my dearest,
  Sing no sad songs for me;
Plant thou no roses at my head,
  Nor shady cypress tree:
Be the green grass above me
  With showers and dewdrops wet:
And if thou wilt, remember,
  And if thou wilt, forget.

I shall not see the shadows,
    I shall not feel the rain;
I shall not hear the nightingale
    Sing on as if in pain:
And dreaming through the twilight
    That doth not rise nor set,
Haply I may remember,
    And haply may forget.

CHRISTINA ROSSETTI

"Oh roses for the flush of youth"

Oh roses for the flush of youth,
    And laurel for the perfect prime;
But pluck an ivy branch for me
    Grown old before my time.

Oh violets for the grave of youth,
    And bay for those dead in their prime;
Give me the withered leaves I chose
    Before in the old time.

CHRISTINA ROSSETTI

A Match

If love were what the rose is,
    And I were like the leaf,
Our lives would grow together
In sad or singing weather,
Blown fields or flowerful closes,
    Green pleasure or grey grief;
If love were what the rose is,
    And I were like the leaf.

If I were what the words are,
    And love were like the tune,
With double sound and single
Delight our lips would mingle,

With kisses glad as birds are
  That get sweet rain at noon;
If I were what the words are,
  And love were like the tune.

If you were life, my darling,
  And I your love were death,
We'd shine and snow together
Ere March made sweet the weather
With daffodil and starling
  And hours of fruitful breath;
If you were life, my darling,
  And I your love were death.

If you were thrall to sorrow,
  And I were page to joy,
We'd play for lives and seasons
With loving looks and treasons
And tears of night and morrow
  And laughs of maid and boy;
If you were thrall to sorrow,
  And I were page to joy.

If you were April's lady,
  And I were lord in May,
We'd throw with leaves for hours
And draw for days with flowers,
Till day like night were shady
  And night were bright like day;
If you were April's lady,
  And I were lord in May.

If you were queen of pleasure,
  And I were king of pain,
We'd hunt love down together,
Pluck out his flying-feather,
And teach his feet a measure,
  And find his mouth a rein;
If you were queen of pleasure,
  And I were king of pain.

ALGERNON CHARLES SWINBURNE

To Lizbie Browne

Dear Lizbie Browne,
Where are you now?
In sun, in rain?—
Or is your brow
Past joy, past pain,
Dear Lizbie Browne?

Sweet Lizbie Browne,
How you could smile,
How you could sing!—
How archly wile
In glance-giving,
Sweet Lizbie Browne!

And, Lizbie Browne,
Who else had hair
Bay-red as yours,
Or flesh as fair
Bred out of doors,
Sweet Lizbie Browne?

When, Lizbie Browne,
You had just begun
To be endeared
By stealth to one,
You disappeared
My Lizbie Browne!

Ay, Lizbie Browne,
So swift your life,
And mine so slow,
You were a wife
Ere I could show
Love, Lizbie Browne.

Still, Lizbie Browne,
You won, they said,
The best of men
When you were wed.

Where went you then,
O Lizbie Browne?

Dear Lizbie Browne,
I should have thought,
"Girls ripen fast,"
And coaxed and caught
You ere you passed,
Dear Lizbie Browne!

But, Lizbie Browne,
I let you slip;
Shaped not a sign;
Touched never your lip
With lip of mine,
Lost Lizbie Browne!

So, Lizbie Browne,
When on a day
Men speak of me
As not, you'll say,
"And who was he?"—
Yes, Lizbie Browne!

THOMAS HARDY

"*Thou didst delight my eyes*"

Thou didst delight my eyes:
Yet who am I? nor first
Nor last nor best, that durst
Once dream of thee for prize;
Nor this the only time
Thou shalt set love to rhyme.

Thou didst delight my ear:
Ah! little praise; thy voice
Makes other hearts rejoice,
Makes all ears glad that hear;
And short my joy: but yet,
O song, do not forget.

For what wert thou to me?
How shall I say? The moon,
That poured her midnight noon
Upon his wrecking sea;—
A sail, that for a day
Has cheered the castaway.

ROBERT BRIDGES

"Loveliest of trees"

Loveliest of trees, the cherry now
Is hung with bloom along the bough,
And stands about the woodland ride
Wearing white for Eastertide.

Now, of my threescore years and ten,
Twenty will not come again,
And take from seventy springs a score,
It only leaves me fifty more.

And since to look at things in bloom
Fifty springs are little room,
About the woodlands I will go
To see the cherry hung with snow.

A. E. HOUSMAN

"When I was one-and-twenty"

When I was one-and-twenty
    I heard a wise man say,
"Give crowns and pounds and guineas
    But not your heart away;
Give pearls away and rubies
    But keep your fancy free."
But I was one-and-twenty,
    No use to talk to me.

When I was one-and-twenty
    I heard him say again,

"The heart out of the bosom
   Was never given in vain;
'Tis paid with sighs a plenty
   And sold for endless rue."
And I am two-and-twenty,
   And oh, 'tis true, 'tis true.

A. E. HOUSMAN

Brown Penny

I whispered, "I am too young,"
And then, "I am old enough";
Wherefore I threw a penny
To find out if I might love.
"Go and love, go and love, young man,
If the lady be young and fair."
Ah, penny, brown penny, brown penny,
I am looped in the loops of her hair.

O love is the crookèd thing,
There is nobody wise enough
To find out all that is in it,
For he would be thinking of love
Till the stars had run away
And the shadows eaten the moon.
Ah, penny, brown penny, brown penny,
One cannot begin it too soon.

WILLIAM BUTLER YEATS

STORY LYRICS

Sir Patrick Spence

The king sits in Dumferling toune,
    Drinking the blude-reid wine:
"O whar will I get guid sailor,
    To sail this ship of mine?"

Up and spak an eldern knicht,
    Sat at the kings richt knee:
"Sir Patrick Spence is the best sailor
    That sails upon the sea."

The king has written a braid letter,
    And signed it wi his hand,
And sent it to Sir Patrick Spence,
    Was walking on the sand.

The first line that Sir Patrick red,
    A loud lauch lauched he;
The next line that Sir Patrick red,
    The teir blinded his ee.

"O wha is this has done this deid,
    This ill deid done to me,
To send me out this time o' the yeir,
    To sail upon the sea!

"Mak haste, mak haste, my mirry men all,
    Our guid ship sails the morne":
"O say na sæ, my master deir,
    For I feir a deadlie storme.

"Late late yestreen I saw the new moone,
    Wi the auld moone in hir arme,
And I feir, I feir, my deir master,
    That we will come to harme."

O our Scots nobles wer richt laith
    To weet thair cork-heild shoone;
But lang owre a' the play wer playd,
    Thair hats they swam aboone.

O lang, lang may thair ladies sit,
   Wi thair fans into thair hand,
Or ere they see Sir Patrick Spence
   Come sailing to the land.

O lang, lang may the ladies stand,
   Wi thair gold kaims in thair hair,
Waiting for thair ain deir lords,
   For they'll see them na mair.

Haf owre, haf owre to Aberdour,
   It's fiftie fadom deip,
And thair lies guid Sir Patrick Spence,
   Wi the Scots lords at his feit.

ANON.

laith = loth: *aboone* = above: *kaims* = combs

The Golden Vanity

It's I've got a ship in the north country,
Down in the Lowlands low,
And I fear she may be took by the Spanish enemy,
As she sails on the Lowland sea,
As she sails in the Lowlands low.

And up then stepped a little cabin boy,
Down in the Lowlands low,
Saying: "What'll you give me if I do them destroy,
And sink them in the Lowland sea,
And sink them in the Lowlands low?"

"Oh, I'll give you silver and likewise gold,
Down in the Lowlands low,
And my only daughter for to be your bride,
If you'll sink them in the Lowland sea,
If you'll sink them in the Lowlands low."

"Oh wrap me up in my black bear skin,
Down in the Lowlands low,
And heave me overboard for to sink or to swim,
And I'll sink them in the Lowland sea,
I'll sink them in the Lowlands low."

Now some was playing cards and the others playing dice,
Down in the Lowlands low,
And the boy had an auger, bored two holes at once,
And he sunk them in the Lowland sea,
And he sunk them in the Lowlands low.

He leaned upon his breast and he swum back again,
Down in the Lowlands low,
Saying: "Master, take me up, for I'm sure I will be slain,
And I've sunk her in the Lowland sea,
And I've sunk her in the Lowlands low."

"I'll not take you up," the master he cried,
  Down in the Lowlands low,
"But I'll shoot you and kill you and send you with the tide,
  And I'll drown you in the Lowland sea,
  And I'll drown you in the Lowlands low."

He leaned upon his breast and swum round the larboard side,
Down in the Lowlands low,
"O messmates, take me up for I fear I will be slain,
And I've sunk her in the Lowland sea,
And I've sunk her in the Lowlands low."

His messmates took him up, and on the deck he died,
Down in the Lowlands low,
And they wrapped him up in an old cow's hide,
And they sunk him in the Lowland sea,
And they sunk him in the Lowlands low.

ANON.

The Wee Wee Man

As I was walking all alone,
    Between a water and a wa,
And there I spy'd a wee wee man,
    And he was the least that ere I saw.

His legs were scarce a shathmont's length,
    And thick and thimber was his thigh;

Between his brows there was a span,
   And between his shoulders there was three.

He took up a meikle stane,
   And he flang't as far as I could see;
Though I had been a Wallace wight,
   I couldna liften 't to my knee.

"O wee wee man, but thou be strang!
   O tell me where thy dwelling be?"
"My dwelling's down at yon bonny bower;
   O will you go with me and see?"

On we lap, and awa we rade,
   Till we came to yon bonny green;
We lighted down for to bait our horse,
   And out there came a lady fine.

Four and twenty at her back,
   And they were a' clad out in green;
Though the King of Scotland had been there,
   The warst o them might hæ been his queen.

On we lap, and awa we rade,
   Till we came to yon bonny ha,
Whare the roof was o the beaten gould,
   And the floor was o the crystal a'.

When we came to the stair-foot,
   Ladies were dancing, jimp and sma,
But in the twinkling of an eye,
   My wee wee man was clean awa.

ANON.

shathmont's length = above six inches: *wight* = strong

Thomas the Rhymer

True Thomas lay on Huntlie bank;
   A ferlie he spied wi' his e'e;
And there he saw a ladye bright
   Come riding down by the Eildon Tree.

Her skirt was o' the grass-green silk,
  Her mantle o' the velvet fyne;
At ilka tett o' her horse's mane
  Hung fifty siller bells and nine.

True Thomas he pu'd aff his cap,
  And louted low down on his knee:
"Hail to thee, Mary, Queen of Heaven!
  For thy peer on earth could never be."

"O no, O no, Thomas," she said,
  "That name does not belang to me;
I'm but the Queen o' fair Elfland,
  That am hither come to visit thee.

"Harp and carp, Thomas," she said;
  "Harp and carp along wi' me;
And if ye dare to kiss my lips,
  Sure of your bodie I will be."

"Betide me weal, betide me woe,
  That weird shall never daunten me."
Syne he has kiss'd her rosy lips,
  All underneath the Eildon Tree.

"Now ye maun go wi' me," she said,
  "True Thomas, ye maun go wi' me;
And ye maun serve me seven years,
  Thro' weal or woe as may chance to be."

She's mounted on her milk-white steed,
  She's ta'en true Thomas up behind;
And aye, whene'er her bridle rang,
  The steed gaed swifter than the wind.

O they rade on, and farther on,
  The steed gaed swifter than the wind;
Until they reach'd a desert wide,
  And living land was left behind.

"Light down, light down now, true Thomas,
  And lean your head upon my knee;

Abide ye there a little space,
 And I will show you ferlies three.

"O see ye not yon narrow road,
 So thick beset wi' thorns and briers?
That is the Path of Righteousness,
 Though after it but few inquires.

"And see ye not yon braid, braid road,
 That lies across the lily leven?
That is the Path of Wickedness,
 Though some call it the Road to Heaven.

"And see ye not yon bonny road
 That winds about the fernie brae?
That is the road to fair Elfland,
 Where thou and I this night maun gæ.

"But, Thomas, ye sall haud your tongue,
 Whatever ye may hear or see;
For speak ye word in Elfyn-land,
 Ye'll ne'er win back to your ain countrie."

O they rade on, and farther on,
 And they waded rivers abune the knee;
And they saw neither sun nor moon,
 But they heard the roaring of the sea.

It was mirk, mirk night, there was næ starlight,
 They waded thro' red blude to the knee;
For a' the blude that's shed on the earth
 Rins through the springs o' that countrie.

Syne they came to a garden green,
 And she pu'ed an apple fræ a tree:
"Take this for thy wages, true Thomas;
 It will give thee the tongue that can never lee."

"My tongue is my ain," true Thomas he said;
 "A gudely gift ye wad gie to me!
I neither dought to buy or sell
 At fair or tryst where I might be.

"I dought neither speak to prince or peer,
    Nor ask of grace from fair ladye!"—
"Now haud thy peace, Thomas," she said,
    "For as I say, so must it be."

He has gotten a coat of the even cloth,
    And a pair o' shoon of the velvet green;
And till seven years were gane and past,
    True Thomas on earth was never seen.

                                        ANON.

ferlies = marvels: *tett* = tuft: *harp and carp* =
play and recite: *leven* = lawn: *dought* = could

La Belle Dame sans Merci

O what can ail thee, knight-at-arms,
    Alone and palely loitering?
The sedge has wither'd from the lake,
    And no birds sing.

O what can ail thee, knight-at-arms!
    So haggard and so woe-begone?
The squirrel's granary is full,
    And the harvest's done.

I see a lily on thy brow,
    With anguish moist and fever dew,
And on thy cheeks a fading rose
    Fast withereth too.

I met a lady in the meads,
    Full beautiful—a færy's child,
Her hair was long, her foot was light,
    And her eyes were wild.

I made a garland for her head,
    And bracelets too, and fragrant zone;
She look'd at me as she did love,
    And made sweet moan.

I set her on my pacing steed,
And nothing else saw all day long,
For sidelong would she bend, and sing
   A færy's song.

She found me roots of relish sweet,
   And honey wild, and manna dew,
And sure in language strange she said—
   "I love thee true."

She took me to her elfin grot,
   And there she wept, and sigh'd full sore,
And there I shut her wild wild eyes
   With kisses four.

And there she lullèd me asleep,
   And there I dream'd—Ah! woe betide!
The latest dream I ever dream'd
   On the cold hill side.

I saw pale kings and princes too,
   Pale warriors, death-pale were they all;
They cried—"La Belle Dame sans Merci
   Hath thee in thrall!"

I saw their starved lips in the gloam,
   With horrid warning gapèd wide,
And I awoke and found me here,
   On the cold hill's side.

And this is why I sojourn here,
   Alone and palely loitering,
Though the sedge has wither'd from the lake,
   And no birds sing.

JOHN KEATS

Dives and Lazarus

As it fell out upon a day,
   Rich Dives he made a feast,
And he invited all his friends
   And gentry of the best.

Then Lazarus laid him down and down,
    And down at Dives' door;
"Some meat, some drink, brother Dives,
    Bestow upon the poor!"—

"Thou art none of my brother, Lazarus,
    That lies begging at my door;
No meat nor drink will I give thee,
    Nor bestow upon the poor."

Then Lazarus laid him down and down,
    And down at Dives' wall,
"Some meat, some drink, brother Dives,
    Or with hunger starve I shall!"—

"Thou art none of my brother, Lazarus,
    That lies begging at my wall;
No meat nor drink will I give thee,
    But with hunger starve you shall."

Then Lazarus laid him down and down,
    And down at Dives' gate:
"Some meat, some drink, brother Dives,
    For Jesus Christ his sake!"—

"Thou art none of my brother, Lazarus,
    That lies begging at my gate;
No meat nor drink will I give thee,
    For Jesus Christ his sake."

Then Dives sent out his merry men,
    To whip poor Lazarus away;
They had no power to strike a stroke,
    But flung their whips away.

Then Dives sent out his hungry dogs,
    To bite him as he lay;
They had no power to bite at all,
    But licked his sores away.

As it fell out upon a day,
    Poor Lazarus sicken'd and died;

Then came two angels out of heaven
His soul therein to guide.

"Rise up, rise up, brother Lazarus,
And go along with me;
For you've a place prepared in heaven,
To sit on an angel's knee."

As it fell out upon a day,
Rich Dives sicken'd and died;
Then came two serpents out of hell,
His soul therein to guide.

"Rise up, rise up, brother Dives,
And go with us to see
A dismal place, prepared in hell,
To sit on a serpent's knee."

Then Dives look'd up with his eyes,
And saw poor Lazarus blest:
"Give me one drop of water, brother Lazarus,
To quench my flaming thirst.

"Oh had I as many years to abide
As there are blades of grass,
Then there would be an end, but now
Hell's pains will ne'er be past!

"Oh was I now but alive again,
The space of one half hour!
Oh that I had my peace secure!
Then the devil should have no power."

ANON.

Edward

"Why does your brand sæ drop wi' blude,
Edward, Edward?
Why does your brand sæ drop wi' blude,

And why sæ sad gang ye, O?"—
"O I hæ kill'd my hawk sæ gude,
    Mither, mither;
  O I hæ kill'd my hawk sæ gude,
    And I had næ mair but he, O."

"Your hawk's blude was never sæ red,
    Edward, Edward;
  Your hawk's blude was never sæ red,
    My dear son, I tell thee, O."—
"O I hæ kill'd my red-roan steed,
    Mither, mither;
  O I hæ kill'd my red-roan steed,
    That erst was sæ fair and free, O."

"Your steed was auld, and ye hæ got mair,
    Edward, Edward;
  Your steed was auld, and ye hæ got mair;
    Some other dule ye dree, O."
"O I hæ kill'd my father dear,
    Mither, mither;
  O I hæ kill'd my father dear,
    Alas, and wæ is me, O!"

"And whatten penance will ye dree for that,
    Edward, Edward?
  Whatten penance will ye dree for that?
    My dear son, now tell me, O,"—
"I'll set my feet in yonder boat,
    Mither, mither;
  "I'll set my feet in yonder boat,
    And I'll fare over the sea, O."

"And what will ye do wi' your tow'rs and your ha',
    Edward, Edward?
  And what will ye do wi' your tow'rs and your ha',
    That were sæ fair to see, O?"—
"I'll let them stand till they doun fa',
    Mither, mither;
  I'll let them stand till they doun fa',
    For here never mair maun I be, O."

"And what will ye leave to your bairns and your wife,
    Edward, Edward?
And what will ye leave to your bairns and your wife,
    When ye gang owre the sea, O?"—
"The warld's room: let them beg through life,
    Mither, mither;
"The warld's room: let them beg through life,
    For them never mair will I see, O."

"And what will ye leave to your ain mither dear,
    Edward, Edward?
And what will ye leave to your ain mither dear,
    My dear son, now tell me, O?"—
"The curse of hell fræ me sall ye bear,
    Mither, mither;
The curse of hell fræ me sall ye bear:
    Sic counsels ye gave to me, O!"

ANON.

brand = sword: dule = sorrow: dree = suffer:
ha' = hall: sall = shall

"Mother, Mother, make my bed"

"Mother, mother, make my bed,
    And wrap me in a milk-white sheet,
    And wrap me in a cloak of gold,
    And see whether I can sleep.

"And send me the two bailies,
    Likewise my sister's son,
    That they may fetch me my own true love,
    Or I shall die before ever he can come."

The first three miles they walked,
    The next three miles they ran,
    Until they came to the high water side,
    And laid on their breast and swam.

They swam till they came to the high castle
Where my lord he was sitting at meat:
"If you did but know what news I brought,
 Not one mouthful more would you eat."

"What news, what news have you brought me?
 Is my castle burnt down?"
"Oh no, your true love is very, very ill,
 And she'll die before ever you can come."

"Saddle me my milk-white horse,
 And bridle him so neat,
 That I may kiss of her lily lips
 That are to me so sweet."

They saddled him his milk-white steed
At twelve o'clock at night.
He rode, he rode till he met six young men
With a corpse all dressed in white.

"Come set her down, come set her down,
 Come set her down by me,
 That I may kiss of her lily, lily lips,
 Before she is taken away."

My lady, she died on the Saturday night
Before the sun went down.
My lord he died on the Sunday following
Before evening prayers began.

My lady she was buried in the high castle
My lord was buried in the choir;
Out of my lady grew a red rose,
And out of my lord a sweet briar.

This rose and the briar they grew up together,
Till they could grow no higher,
They met at the top in a true lover's knot,
And the rose it clung round the sweet briar.

                                        ANON.

The Twa Corbies

As I was walking all alane,
I heard twa corbies making a mane:
The tane unto the tither did say,
"Whar sall we gang and dine the day?"

"—In behint yon auld fail dyke
I wot there lies a new-slain knight;
And næbody kens that he lies there
But his hawk, his hound, and his lady fair.

"His hound is to the hunting gane,
His hawk to fetch the wild-fowl hame,
His lady's ta'en anither mate,
So we may mak' our dinner sweet.

"Ye'll sit on his white hause-bane,
And I'll pike out his bonny blue e'en:
Wi' æ lock o' his gowden hair
We'll theek our nest when it grows bare.

"Mony a one for him maks mane,
But nane sall ken whar he is gane:
O'er his white banes, when they are bare,
The wind sall blaw for evermair."

ANON.

corbies = crows: *fail* = turf
hause-bane = neckbone: *theek* = thatch

Bonnie George Campbell

Hie upon Hielands,
    and laigh upon Tay,
Bonnie George Campbell
    rode out on a day.

He saddled, he bridled,
    and gallant rode he,

And hame cam his guid horse,
    but never cam he.

Out cam his mother dear,
    greeting fu sair,
And out cam his bonnie bryde,
    riving her hair.

"The meadow lies green,
    the corn is unshorn,
But bonnie George Campbell
    will never return."

Saddled and bridled
    and booted rode he,
A plume in his helmet,
    A sword at his knee.

But toom cam his saddle,
    all bloody to see,
Oh, hame cam his guid horse,
    but never cam he!

ANON.

laigh = low: *greeting* = weeping
toom = empty

The Bonny Earl o'Moray

Ye Highlands and ye Lawlands,
    O where hae ye been?
They hae slain the Earl o' Moray,
    And hae laid him on the green.

Now wae be to thee, Huntley!
    And whairfore did ye sae!
I bade you bring him wi' you,
    But forbade you him to slay.

He was a braw gallant,
    And he rid at the ring;

And the bonny Earl o' Moray,
  O he might hae been a king!

He was a braw gallant,
  And he play'd at the ba';
And the bonny Earl o' Moray
  Was the flower amang them a'.

He was a braw gallant,
  And he play'd at the gluve;
And the bonny Earl o' Moray,
  O he was the Queen's luve!

O lang will his Lady
  Look owre the Castle Downe,
Ere she see the Earl o' Moray
  Come sounding through the town!

ANON.

Helen of Kirkconnell

I wish I were where Helen lies,
Night and day on me she cries;
O that I were where Helen lies,
  On fair Kirkconnell lea!

Curst be the heart that thought the thought,
And curst the hand that fired the shot,
When in my arms burd Helen dropt,
  And died to succour me!

O think na ye my heart was sair,
When my Love dropp'd and spak næ mair!
There did she swoon wi' meikle care,
  On fair Kirkconnell lea;

As I went down the water side,
None but my foe to be my guide,
None but my foe to be my guide,
  On fair Kirkconnell lea;

I lighted down my sword to draw,
I hacked him in pieces sma',
I hacked him in pieces sma',
   For her sake that died for me.

O Helen fair, beyond compare!
I'll mak a garland o' thy hair,
Shall bind my heart for evermair,
   Until the day I dee!

O that I were where Helen lies!
Night and day on me she cries;
Out of my bed she bids me rise,
   Says, "Haste, and come to me!"

O Helen fair! O Helen chaste!
If I were with thee, I'd be blest,
Where thou lies low an' taks thy rest,
   On fair Kirkconnell lea.

I wish my grave were growing green,
A winding-sheet drawn owre my een,
And I in Helen's arms lying,
   On fair Kirkconnell lea.

I wish I were where Helen lies!
Night and day on me she cries;
And I am weary of the skies,
   For her sake that died for me.

ANON.

The Unquiet Grave

"The wind doth blow today, my love,
   And a few small drops of rain;
I never had but one true-love;
   In cold grave she was lain.

"I'll do as much for my true-love
   As any young man may;

I'll sit and mourn all at her grave
For a twelvemonth and a day."

The twelvemonth and a day being up,
The dead began to speak:
"Oh who sits weeping on my grave,
And will not let me sleep?"

" 'Tis I, my love, sits on your grave,
And will not let you sleep;
For I crave one kiss of your clay-cold lips,
And that is all I seek."

"You crave one kiss of my clay-cold lips;
But my breath smells earthy strong;
If you have one kiss of my clay-cold lips,
Your time will not be long.

" 'Tis down in yonder garden green,
Love, where we used to walk,
The finest flower that ere was seen
Is wither'd to a stalk.

"The stalk is wither'd dry, my love,
So will our hearts decay;
So make yourself content, my love,
Till God calls you away."

ANON.

The Grey Cock

"I must be going, no longer staying,
The burning Thames I have to cross.
Oh, I must be guided without a stumble
Into the arms of my dear lass."

When he came to his true love's window,
He knelt down gently on a stone,
And it's through a pane he whispered slowly:
"My dear girl, are you alone?"

She rose her head from her down-soft pillow,
And snowy were her milk-white breasts,
Saying: "Who's there, who's there at my bedroom window,
Disturbing me from my long night's rest?"

"Oh, I'm your love and don't discover,
I pray you rise, love, and let me in,
For I am fatigued from my long night's journey.
Besides, I am wet into the skin."

Now this young girl rose and put on her clothing.
She quickly let her own true love in.
Oh, they kissed, shook hands, and embraced together,
Till that long night was near an end.

"O Willie dear, O dearest Willie,
Where is that colour you'd some time ago?"
"O Mary dear, the clay has changed me.
I'm but the ghost of your Willie O."

"Then O cock, O cock, O handsome cockerel,
I pray you not crow until it is day.
For your wings I'll make of the very first beaten gold,
And your comb I'll make of the silver grey."

But the cock it crew, and it crew so fully.
It crew three hours before it was day.
And before it was day, my love had to go away.
Not by the light of the moon or the light of day.

Then it's "Willie dear, O dearest Willie,
Whenever shall I see you again?"
"When the fish they fly, love, and the sea runs dry, love,
And the rocks they melt in the heat of the sun."

ANON.

The Brown Girl

"I am as brown as brown can be,
    And my eyes as black as sloe;
I am as brisk as brisk can be,
    And wild as forest doe.

"My love he was so high and proud,
    His fortune too so high,
He for another fair pretty maid
    Me left and passed me by.

"Me did he send a love-letter,
    He sent it from the town,
Saying no more he loved me,
    For that I was so brown.

"I sent his letter back again,
    Saying his love I valued not,
Whether that he would fancy me,
    Whether that he would not.

"When that six months were overpassed,
    Were overpassed and gone,
Then did my lover, once so bold,
    Lie on his bed and groan.

"When that six months were overpassed,
    Were gone and overpassed,
O then my lover, once so bold,
    With love was sick at last.

"First sent he for the doctor-man:
    'You, doctor, me must cure;
The pains that now do torture me
    I can not long endure.'

"Next did he send from out the town,
    O next did send for me;
He sent for me, the brown, brown girl
    Who once his wife should be.

"O neer a bit the doctor-man
    His sufferings could relieve;
O never an one but the brown, brown girl
    Who could his life reprieve."

Now you shall hear what love she had
    For this poor love-sick man,

How all one day, a summer's day,
   She walked and never ran.

When that she came to his bedside,
   Where he lay sick and weak,
O then for laughing she could not stand
   Upright upon her feet.

"You flouted me, you scouted me,
   And many another one;
Now the reward is come at last,
   For all that you have done."

The rings she took from off her hands,
   The rings by two and three:
"O take, O take these golden rings,
   By them remember me."

She had a white wand in her hand,
   She strake him on the breast:
"My faith and troth I give back to thee,
   So may thy soul have rest."

"Prithee," said he, "forget, forget,
   Prithee forget, forgive;
O grant me yet a little space,
   That I may be well and live."

"O never will I forget, forgive,
   So long as I have breath;
I'll dance above your green, green grave
   Where you do lie beneath."

ANON.

"Johnny, I hardly knew ye"

While going the road to sweet Athy,
   Hurroo! hurroo!
While going the road to sweet Athy,
   Hurroo! hurroo!

While going the road to sweet Athy,
A stick in my hand and a drop in my eye,
A doleful damsel I heard cry:
          "Och, Johnny, I hardly knew ye!

    "With drums and guns, and guns and drums,
      The enemy nearly slew ye;
      My darling dear, you look so queer,
      Och, Johnny, I hardly knew ye!

"Where are your eyes that looked so mild?
          Hurroo! hurroo!
Where are your eyes that looked so mild?
          Hurroo! hurroo!
Where are your eyes that looked so mild?
When my poor heart you first beguiled?
Why did you run from me and the child?
    Och, Johnny, I hardly knew ye!
      With drums, etc.

"Where are the legs with which you run?
          Hurroo! hurroo!
Where are the legs with which you run?
          Hurroo! hurroo!
Where are the legs with which you run
When first you went to carry a gun?
Indeed, your dancing days are done!
    Och, Johnny, I hardly knew ye!
      With drums, etc.

"It grieved my heart to see you sail,
          Hurroo! hurroo!
It grieved my heart to see you sail,
          Hurroo! hurroo!
It grieved my heart to see you sail,
Though from my heart you took leg-bail;
Like a cod you're doubled up head and tail,
    Och, Johnny, I hardly knew ye!
      With drums, etc.

"You haven't an arm and you haven't a leg,
          Hurroo! hurroo!

You haven't an arm and you haven't a leg,
    Hurroo! hurroo!
You haven't an arm and you haven't a leg,
You're an eyeless, noseless, chickenless egg;
You'll have to be put with a bowl to beg:
    Och, Johnny, I hardly knew ye!
        With drums, etc.

"I'm happy for to see you home,
    Hurroo! hurroo!
I'm happy for to see you home,
    Hurroo! hurroo!
I'm happy for to see you home,
All from the Island of Sulloon;
So low in flesh, so high in bone;
    Och, Johnny, I hardly knew ye!
        With drums, etc.

"But sad it is to see you so,
    Hurroo! hurroo!
But sad it is to see you so,
    Hurroo! hurroo!
But sad it is to see you so,
And to think of you now as an object of woe,
Your Peggy'll still keep ye on as her beau;
    Och, Johnny, I hardly knew ye!

    "With drums and guns, and guns and drums,
    The enemy nearly slew ye;
    My darling dear, you look so queer,
        Och, Johnny, I hardly knew ye!"

                                        ANON.

took leg-bail = ran away

from
Marmion

But as they left the dark'ning heath,
More desperate grew the strife of death.
The English shafts in vollies hailed,
In headlong charge their horse assailed;

Front, flank, and rear, the squadrons sweep,
To break the Scottish circle deep,
  That fought around their king.
But yet, though thick the shafts as snow,
Though charging knights like whirlwinds go,
Though bill-men ply the ghastly blow,
  Unbroken was the ring;
Each stepping where his comrade stood,
  The instant that he fell.
No thought was there of dastard flight;—
Linked in the serried phalanx tight,
Groom fought like noble, squire like knight,
  As fearlessly and well;
Till utter darkness closed her wing
O'er their thin host and wounded king.
Then skilful Surrey's sage commands
Led back from strife his shattered bands;
  And from the charge they drew,
As mountain-waves, from wasted lands,
  Sweep back to ocean blue.
Then did their loss his foemen know;
Their king, their lords, their mightiest, low,
They melted from the field as snow,
When streams are swoln and south winds blow,
  Dissolves in silent dew.
Tweed's echoes heard the ceaseless plash,
  While many a broken band,
Disordered, through her currents dash,
  To gain the Scottish land;
To town and tower, to down and dale,
To tell red Flodden's dismal tale,
And raise the universal wail.
Tradition, legend, tune, and song,
Shall many an age that wail prolong:
Still from the sire the son shall hear
Of the stern strife, and carnage drear,
  Of Flodden's fatal field,
Where shivered was fair Scotland's spear,
  And broken was her shield!

                          SIR WALTER SCOTT

bill-men = men armed with an ax-head on a long shaft.

The Boys of Wexford

In comes the captain's daughter, the captain of the yeos,
Saying "Brave United Men, we'll ne'er again be foes:
A thousand pounds I'll give you and fly from home with thee;
I'll dress myself in man's attire and fight for liberty."
    We are the Boys of Wexford who fought with heart and hand,
    To burst in twain the galling chain and free our native land.

And when we left our cabins, boys, we left with right good will,
To join our friends and neighbours encamped on Vinegar Hill;
A young man from our ranks a cannon he let go;
He slapped it into Lord Mountjoy—a tryant he laid low.
    We are the Boys of Wexford who fought with heart and hand,
    To burst in twain the galling chain and free our native land.

At Three Rocks and Tubberneering how well we won the day,
Depending on the long bright pike, and well it worked its way:
At Wexford and at Oulart we made them quake with fear;
For every man could do his part like Forth and Shelmaliere.
    We are the Boys of Wexford who fought with heart and hand,
    To burst in twain the galling chain and free our native land.

My curse upon all drinking—'twas that that brought us down;
It lost us Ross and Wexford, and many other town.
And if for want of leaders we lost at Vinegar Hill,
We're ready for another fight and love our country still.
    We are the Boys of Wexford who fought with heart and hand,
    To burst in twain the galling chain and free our native land.

ANON.

yeos = yeomen

The Rose Tree

"O words are lightly spoken,"
  Said Pearse to Connolly,
"Maybe a breath of politic words
  Has withered our Rose Tree;
Or maybe but a wind that blows
  Across the bitter sea."

"It needs to be but watered,"
James Connolly replied,
"To make the green come out again
And spread on every side,
And shake the blossom from the bud
To be the garden's pride."

"But where can we draw water,"
Said Pearse to Connolly,
"When all the wells are parched away?
O plain as plain can be
There's nothing but our own red blood
Can make a right Rose Tree."

WILLIAM BUTLER YEATS

The Foggy Dew

When I was a batchelor early and young,
I followed the weaving trade,
And all the harm ever I done,
Was courting a servant maid.
I courted her the summer season,
And part of the winter too,
And many a night I rolled her in my arms,
All over the Foggy dew.

One night as I lay on my bed,
As I laid fast asleep,
There came a pretty fair maid,
And most bitterly did weep.
She wept she mourned she tore her hair,
Crying, alas what shall I do,
This night I'm resolved to come to bed with you
For fear of the Foggy dew.

It was in the first part of the night,
We both did sport and play,
And in the latter part of the night,
She slept in my arms till day.

When broad day-light did appear,
   She cried I am undone,
Hold your tongue you foolish girl,
   The Foggy dew is gone.

Suppose that we should have a child,
   It would cause us to smile,
Suppose that we should have another
   It would make us laugh awhile.
Suppose that we should have another,
   And another one too,
Would make you leave off your foolish tricks
   And think no more of the Foggy dew.

I love this young girl dearly,
   I loved her as my life,
Took this girl and married her,
   And made her my lawful wife.
Never told her of her faults,
   Nor never intend to do,
But every time she winks or smiles,
   She thinks of the Foggy dew.

ANON.

The Banks of Sweet Primroses

As I walked out one midsummer's morning,
To view the fields and to take the air,
Down by the banks of the sweet primroses,
There I beheld a most lovely fair.

I said: "Fair maid, where can you be a-going,
And what's the occasion of all your grief?
I'll make you as happy as any lady,
If you will grant me one small relief."

"Stand off, stand off, thou false deceiver!
You're a false deceitful man, 'tis plain.

'Tis you that is causing my poor heart to wander,
And to give me comfort is all in vain.

"Now I'll go down to some lonesome valley,
   Where no man on earth there shall me find,
Where the pretty small birds do change their voices,
And every moment blows blusterous wind."

ANON.

"O waly, waly"

O waly, waly up the bank,
   And waly, waly down the bræ,
And waly, waly by yon burnside
   Where I and my Love wont to gæ.
I leant my back against an aik,
   I thought it was a trusty tree;
But first it bow'd and syne it brak:
   Sæ my true Love did lichtly me.

O waly, waly, but love is bonny
   A little time while it is new;
But when 'tis auld, it waxeth cauld
   And fades awa' like morning dew.
O wherefore should I busk my head?
   O wherefore should I kame my hair?
For my true Love has me forsook,
   And says he'll never lo'e me mair.

Now Arthur's Seat sall be my bed,
   The sheets sall ne'er be prest by me;
Saint Anton's Well sall be my drink,
   Since my true Love's forsaken me.
Mart'mas wind, when wilt thou blaw
   And shake the green leaves aff the tree?
O gentle Death, when wilt thou come?
   For of my life I am wearie.

'Tis not the frost, that freezes fell,
   Nor blawing snaw's inclemencie,

'Tis not sic cauld that makes me cry,
   But my Love's heart grown cauld to me.
When we came in by Glasgow town
   We were a comely sight to see:
My Love was clad in the black velvet,
   And I myself in cramasie.

But had I wist, before I kist,
   That love had been sæ ill to win,
I had lockt my heart in a case of gowd
   And pinn'd it with a siller pin.
And O! if my young babe were born,
   And set upon the nurse's knee,
And I myself were dead and gane,
   And the green grass growing over me.

                                        ANON.

lichtly = lightly: *cramasie* = crimson cloth

"I know where I'm going"

I know where I'm going,
I know who's going with me,
I know who I love,
But the dear knows who I'll marry.

I'll have stockings of silk,
Shoes of fine green leather,
Combs to buckle my hair
And a ring for every finger.

Feather beds are soft,
Painted rooms are bonny;
But I'd leave them all
To go with my love Johnny.

Some say he's dark,
I say he's bonny,
He's the flower of them all
My handsome, coaxing Johnny.

I know where I'm going,
I know who's going with me,
I know who I love,
But the dear knows who I'll marry.

ANON.

"I sowed the seeds of love"

I sowed the seeds of love,
And I sowed them in the spring:
I gathered them up in the morning so soon,
While the small birds so sweetly sing.

My garden was planted well
With flowers everywhere:
But I had not the liberty to choose for myself
Of the flowers that I love so dear.

The gardener was standing by;
And I asked him to choose for me.
He chose for me the Violet, the Lily, and the Pink,
But those I refused all three.

The Violet I did not like,
Because it bloomed so soon.
The Lily and the Pink I really overthink,
So I vowed that I would wait till June.

In June there was a red Rosebud,
And that is the flower for me.
I oftentimes have plucked that red Rosebud
Till I gained the willow tree.

The willow tree will twist,
And the willow tree will twine;
I oftentimes have wished I were in that young man's arms,
That once had the heart of mine.

Come all you false young men,
Do not leave me here to complain:
For the grass that has oftentimes been trampled under foot.
Give it time, it will rise again.

ANON.

Polly Perkins

I am a broken-hearted milkman, in grief I'm arrayed,
Through keeping of the company of a young servant maid,
Who lived on board wages to keep the house clean
In a gentleman's family near Paddington Green.

Chorus

She was as beautiful as a butterfly
And as proud as a Queen
Was pretty Polly Perkins of
Paddington Green.

Her eyes were as black as the pips of a pear,
No rose in the garden with her cheeks could compare,
Her hair hung in ringlets so beautiful and long,
I thought that she loved me but I found I was wrong.

When I asked her to marry me she said Oh! what stuff,
And told me to drop it, for she had quite enough
Of my nonsense—at the same time I'd been very kind,
But to marry a milkman she did not feel inclined.

Oh, the man that has me must have silver and gold,
A chariot to ride in and be handsome and bold,
His hair must be curly as any watch spring,
And his whiskers as long as a brush for clothing.

In six months she married, this hard-hearted girl,
But it was not a wicount, and it was not a nearl,
It was not a baronite, but a shade or two wuss,
It was a bow-legged conductor of a Twopenny Bus.

ANON.

The Sandgate Girl's Lamentation

I was a young maid truly,
And lived in Sandgate Street.
I thought to marry a good man
To keep me warm at neet.

He's an ugly body, a bubbly body,
An ill-fared, hideous loon;
And I have married a keelman,
And my good days are done.

I thought to marry a parson
To hear me say my prayers:
But I have married a keelman
And he kicks me down the stairs.

I thought to marry a dyer
To die my apron blue;
But I have married a keelman
And he makes me sorely rue.

I thought to marry a joiner
To make me chair and stool;
But I have married a keelman,
And he's a perfect fool.

I thought to marry a sailor
To bring me sugar and tea;
But I have married a keelman
And that he lets me see.

He's an ugly body, a bubbly body,
An ill-fared, hideous loon;
And I have married a keelman,
And my good days are done.

ANON.

keelman = a boatman on a coal-carrying craft

The Plodder Seam

The Plodder Seam is a wicked seam,
   It's worse than the Trencherbone.
It's hot and there's three foot of shale between
   The coal and rocky stone.
You can smell the smoke from the fires of hell
   Deep under Ashton town.
Oh, the Plodder Seam is a wicked seam,
   It's a mile and a quarter down.

Thirteen hundred tons a day
   Are taken from that mine.
There's a ton of dirt for a ton of coal,
   And a gallon of sweat and grime.
We crawl behind the cutters and
   We scrabble for the coal.
Oh, I'd rather sweep the streets than have
   To burrow like a mole.

ANON.

Blaydon Races

Aa went te Blaydon Races, 'twas on the ninth o' June,
Eighteen hundred an' sixty two on a summer's afternoon.
Aa tyuk the bus fra Balmbra's, an' she wes heavy laden;
Away we went alang Collingwood Street, that's on the road to Blay-
      don.

   Oh, lads, ye shud a' seen us gannin,
   Passin the folks upon the road, just as they were stannin.
   Thor wes lots o' lads an' lasses there, aal wi' smilin faces,
   Gannin alang the Scotswood Road te see the Blaydon Races.

We flew past Airmstrang's factory, an' up te the *Robin Adair*.
Just gannin doon te the railway bridge, the bus-wheel flew off there.
The lasses lost thor petticoats off, an' the veils that hide thor faces;
Aa got two black eyes an' a broken nose in gan te Blaydon Races.

When we gat the wheel put on, away we went agyen,
But them that had thor noses broke, they came back ower hyem.
Some went te the dispensary, an' some te Dr. Gibbs,
An' some te the infirmary, te mend thor broken ribs.

Noo when we gat te Paradise, thor wes bonny gam begun.
Thor wes fower an' twenty on the bus, man, hoo they danced an' sung!
They caalled on me te sing a song, aa sang them *Paddy Fagan;*
Aa danced a jig an' swung me twig, that day aa went te Blaydon.

We flew across the Chain Bridge reet into Blaydon toon,
The bellman he was caalin there, they caalled him Jacky Broon.
Aa saw him taakin te some cheps, an' them he was persuadin
Te gan an' see George Ridley's show in the Mechanic's Haall at Blay-
    don.

The rain it poored aall the day, an' myed the groonds quite muddy.
Coffy John had a white hat on—they yelled: "Whe stole the cuddy?"
Thor wes spice staals an' monkey shows an' aad wives sellin ciders,
An' a chep wi' a ha'penny roondaboot shooting: "Noo, me lads, for
    riders!"

 Oh, lads, ye shud a' seen us gannin,
 Passin the folks upon the road, just as they were stannin.
 Thor wes lots o' lads an' lasses there, aall wi' smilin faces,
 Gannin alang the Scotswood Road te see the Blaydon Races.

ANON.

Bartleme Fair

 While gentlefolks strut in their silver and satins,
 We poor folks that tramp it in straw hats and pattens,
 As merrily old English ballads can sing-o,
 As they in their opperores' outlandish lingo;
 Calling out, bravo, encoro, and caro,
 Though I will sing nothing but Bartleme Fair-o.

 Here first of all, crowds against other crowds driving,
 Like wind and tide meeting, each contrary striving;
 Here's fiddling and fluting, and shouting and shrieking,

Fifes, trumpets, drums, bag-pipes, and barrow-girls squeaking;
My ware round and sound, here's a choice of fine ware-o,
Though all is not sound bought at Bartleme Fair-o.

Here are drolls, hornpipe dancing, and showing of postures;
Plum-porridge, black puddings, and op'ning of oysters;
The tap-house guests swearing, and gall'ry folks squalling,
With salt-boxes, solos, and mouth-pieces bawling;
Pimps, pick-pockets, strollers, fat landladies, sailors,
Bawds, bullies, jilts, jockies, thieves, tumblers, and tailors.

Here's Punch's whole play of the gunpowder-plot, Sir,
Wild beasts all alive, and pease-porridge hot, Sir:
Fine sausages fried, and the Black on the wire;
The whole court of France, and nice pig at the fire.
The ups-and-downs, who'll take a seat in the chair-o?
There are more ups-and-downs than at Bartleme Fair-o.

Here's Whittington's cat, and the tall dromedary,
The chaise without horses, and Queen of Hungary;
The merry-go-rounds, come who rides? come who rides?
Wine, beer, ale, and cakes, fire-eating besides;
The famed learnèd dog that can tell all his letters,
And some men, as scholars, are not much his betters.

This world's a wide fair, where we ramble 'mong gay things;
Our passions, like children, are tempted by play-things;
By sound and by show, by trash and by trumpery,
The fal-lals of fashion, and Frenchified frumpery.
Life is but a droll, rather wretched than rare-o,
And thus ends the ballad of Bartleme Fair-o.

                              GEORGE ALEXANDER STEVENS

Cockles and Mussels

In Dublin's fair city, where the girls are so pretty,
I first set my eyes on sweet Mollie Malone,
As she wheeled her wheel-barrow through streets
                              broad and narrow,
Crying. "Cockles and mussels: alive, alive O!"

She was a fishmonger, but sure 'twas no wonder,
For so were her father and mother before;
They wheeled a wheel-barrow through streets broad
                              and narrow,
Crying, "Cockles and mussels: alive, alive O!

She died of a fever, and no one could save her,
And that was the end of sweet Mollie Malone;
Now a ghost wheels her barrow through streets
                              broad and narrow,
Crying, "Cockles and mussels: alive, alive O!"

                                        ANON.

Meg Merrilees

Old Meg she was a Gipsey,
    And liv'd upon the moors;
Her bed it was the brown heath turf,
    And her house was out of doors.

Her apples were swart blackberries,
    Her currants, pods o' broom;
Her wine was dew of the wild white rose,
    Her book a churchyard tomb.

Her brothers were the craggy hills,
    Her sisters larchen trees;
Alone with her great family
    She liv'd as she did please.

No breakfast had she many a morn,
    No dinner many a noon,
And, 'stead of supper, she would stare
    Full hard against the moon.

    She made her garlanding,
But every morn, of woodbine fresh
And, every night, the dark glen yew
    She wove, and she would sing.

And with her fingers, old and brown,
   She plaited mats o' rushes,
And gave them to the cottagers
   She met among the bushes.

Old Meg was brave as Margaret Queen
   And tall as Amazon;
An old red blanket cloak she wore,
   A chip hat had she on.
God rest her agèd bones somewhere!
   She died full long agone!

JOHN KEATS

The Castaway

Obscurest night involv'd the sky,
   Th' Atlantic billows roar'd,
When such a destin'd wretch as I,
   Wash'd headlong from on board,
Of friends, of hope, of all bereft,
His floating home for ever left.

No braver chief could Albion boast
   Than he with whom he went,
Nor ever ship left Albion's coast,
   With warmer wishes sent.
He lov'd them both, but both in vain,
Nor him beheld, nor her again.

Not long beneath the whelming brine,
   Expert to swim, he lay;
Nor soon he felt his strength decline,
   Or courage die away;
But wag'd with death a lasting strife,
Supported by despair of life.

He shouted: nor his friends had fail'd
   To check the vessel's course,
But so the furious blast prevail'd,
   That, pitiless perforce,

They left their outcast mate behind,
And scudded still before the wind.

Some succour yet they could afford;
    And such as storms allow,
The cask, the coop, the floated cord,
    Delay'd not to bestow.
But he (they knew) nor ship, nor shore,
Whate'er they gave, should visit more.

Nor, cruel as it seemed, could he
    Their haste himself condemn,
Aware that flight, in such a sea,
    Alone could rescue them;
Yet bitter felt it still to die
Deserted, and his friends so nigh.

He long survives, who lives an hour
    In ocean, self-upheld;
And so long he, with unspent pow'r,
    His destiny repell'd;
And ever, as the minutes flew,
Entreated help, or cried—Adieu!

At length, his transient respite past,
    His comrades, who before
Had heard his voice in ev'ry blast,
    Could catch the sound no more.
For then, by toil subdued, he drank
The stifling wave, and then he sank.

No poet wept him: but the page
    Of narrative sincere,
That tells his name, his worth, his age,
    Is wet with Anson's tear.
And tears by bards or heroes shed
Alike immortalize the dead.

I therefore purpose not, or dream,
    Descanting on his fate,
To give the melancholy theme
    A more enduring date:

But misery still delights to trace
Its 'semblance in another's case.

No voice divine the storm allay'd,
    No light propitious shone;
When, snatch'd from all effectual aid,
    We perished, each alone:
But I beneath a rougher sea,
And whelm'd in deeper gulphs than he.

WILLIAM COWPER

from
Sir Eustace Grey

Then those ill-favour'd Ones, whom none
    But my unhappy eyes could view,
Led me, with wild emotion, on,
    And,with resistless terror, drew.
Through lands we fled, o'er seas we flew,
    And halted on a boundless plain;
Where nothing fed, nor breathed, nor grew,
    But silence ruled the still domain.

Upon that boundless plain, below,
    The setting sun's last rays were shed,
And gave a mild and sober glow,
    Where all were still, asleep, or dead;
Vast ruins in the midst were spread,
    Pillars and pediments sublime,
Where the gray moss had form'd a bed,
    And clothed the crumbling spoils of time.

There was I fix'd, I know not how,
    Condemn'd for untold years to stay:
Yet years were not;—one dreadful *now*
    Endured no change of night or day;
The same mild evening's sleeping ray
    Shone softly-solemn and serene,
And all that time I gazed away,
    The setting sun's sad rays were seen.

At length a moment's sleep stole on,—
    Again came my commission'd foes;
Again through sea and land we're gone,
    No peace, no respite, no repose:
Above the dark broad sea we rose,
    We ran through bleak and frozen land;
I had no strength their strength t'oppose,
    An infant in a giant's hand.

They placed me where those streamers play,
    Those nimble beams of brilliant light;
It would the stoutest heart dismay,
    To see, to feel, that dreadful sight:
So swift, so pure, so cold, so bright,
    They pierced my frame with icy wound,
And all that half-year's polar night,
    Those dancing streamers wrapp'd me round.

Slowly that darkness pass'd away,
    When down upon the earth I fell,—
Some hurried sleep was mine by day;
    But, soon as toll'd the evening bell,
They forced me on, where ever dwell
    Far-distant men in cities fair,
Cities of whom no trav'lers tell,
    Nor feet but mine were wanderers there.

Their watchmen stare, and stand aghast,
    As on we hurry through the dark;
The watch-light blinks as we go past,
    The watch-dog shrinks and fears to bark;
The watch-tower's bell sounds shrill; and, hark!
    The free wind blows—we've left the town—
A wide sepulchral ground I mark,
    And on a tombstone place me down.

What monuments of mighty dead!
    What tombs of various kinds are found!
And stones erect their shadows shed
    On humble graves, with wickers bound;
Some risen fresh, above the ground,
    Some level with the native clay,

What sleeping millions wait the sound,
 "Arise, ye dead, and come away!"

Alas! they stay not for that call;
 Spare me this woe! ye demons, spare!—
They come! the shrouded shadows all,—
 'Tis more than mortal brain can bear;
Rustling they rise, they sternly glare
 At man upheld by vital breath;
Who, led by wicked fiends, should dare
 To join the shadowy troops of death!

Yes, I have felt all man can feel,
 Till he pays his nature's debt;
Ills that no hope has strength to heal,
 No mind the comfort to forget:
Whatever cares the heart can fret,
 The spirits wear, the temper gall,
Woe, want, dread, anguish, all beset
 My sinful soul!—together all!

Those fiends upon a shaking fen
 Fix'd me, in dark tempestuous night;
There never trod the foot of men,
 There flock'd the fowl in wint'ry flight;
There danced the moor's deceitful light
 Above the pool where sedges grow;
And when the morning-sun shone bright,
 It shone upon a field of snow.

They hung me on a bough so small,
 The rook could build her nest no higher;
They fix'd me on the trembling ball
 That crowns the steeple's quiv'ring spire;
They set me where the seas retire,
 But drown with their returning tide;
And made me flee the mountain's fire,
 When rolling from its burning side.

GEORGE CRABBE

Meeting at Night

The grey sea and the long black land;
And the yellow half-moon large and low;
And the startled little waves that leap
In fiery ringlets from their sleep,
As I gain the cove with pushing prow,
And quench its speed i' the slushy sand.

Then a mile of warm sea-scented beach;
Three fields to cross till a farm appears;
A tap at the pane, the quick sharp scratch
And blue spurt of a lighted match,
And a voice less loud, thro' its joys and fears,
Than the two hearts beating each to each!

ROBERT BROWNING

Confessions

What is he buzzing in my ears?
  "Now that I come to die,
Do I view the world as a vale of tears?"
  Ah, reverend sir, not I!

What I viewed there once, what I view again
  Where the physic bottles stand
On the table's edge,—is a suburb lane,
  With a wall to my bedside hand.

That lane sloped, much as the bottles do,
  From a house you could descry
O'er the garden-wall: is the curtain blue
  Or green to a healthy eye?

To mine, it serves for the old June weather
  Blue above lane and wall;
And that farthest bottle labelled "Ether"
  Is the house o'ertopping all.

At a terrace, somewhere near the stopper,
  There watched for me, one June,

A girl: I know, sir, it's improper,
  My poor mind's out of tune.

Only, there was a way . . . you crept
  Close by the side, to dodge
Eyes in the house, two eyes except:
  They styled their house "The Lodge."

What right had a lounger up their lane?
  But, by creeping very close,
With the good wall's help,—their eyes might strain
  And stretch themselves to Oes,

Yet never catch her and me together,
  As she left the attic, there,
By the rim of the bottle labelled "Ether,"
  And stole from stair to stair,

And stood by the rose-wreathed gate. Alas,
  We loved, sir—used to meet:
How sad and bad and mad it was—
  But then, how it was sweet!

                              ROBERT BROWNING

The Azalea

There, where the sun shines first
Against our room,
She train'd the gold Azalea, whose perfume
She, Spring-like, from her breathing grace dispersed.
Last night the delicate crests of saffron bloom,
For this their dainty likeness watch'd and nurst,
Were just at point to burst.
At dawn I dream'd, O God, that she was dead,
And groan'd aloud upon my wretched bed,
And waked, ah, God, and did not waken her,
But lay, with eyes still closed,
Perfectly bless'd in the delicious sphere
By which I knew so well that she was near,
My heart to speechless thankfulness composed.

Till 'gan to stir
A dizzy somewhat in my troubled head—
It *was* the azalea's breath, and she *was* dead!
The warm night had the lingering buds disclosed,
And I had fall'n asleep with to my breast
A chance-found letter press'd
In which she said,
"So, till tomorrow eve, my Own, adieu!
Parting's well-paid with soon again to meet,
Soon in your arms to feel so small and sweet,
Sweet to myself that am so sweet to you!"

COVENTRY PATMORE

The Foreboding

Looking by chance in at the open window
   I saw my own self seated in his chair
With gaze abstracted, furrowed forehead,
   Unkempt hair.

I thought that I had suddenly come to die,
   That to a cold corpse this was my farewell,
Until the pen moved slowly on the paper
   And tears fell.

He had written a name, yours, in printed letters
   One word on which bemusedly to pore:
No protest, no desire, your naked name,
   Nothing more.

Would it be tomorrow, would it be next year?
   But the vision was not false, this much I knew;
And I turned angrily from the open window
   Aghast at you.

Why never a warning, either by speech or look,
   That the love you cruelly gave me could not last?
Already it was too late: the bait swallowed,
   The hook fast.

ROBERT GRAVES

LYRICAL POEMS

"Is it possible?"

Is it possible
That so high debate,
So sharp, so sore, and of such rate,
Should end so soon that was begun so late,
    Is it possible?

Is it possible?
So cruel intent,
So hasty heat and so soon spent,
From love to hate, and thence for to relent,
    Is it possible?

Is it possible
That any may find
Within one heart so divers mind,
To change or turn as weather and wind,
    Is it possible?

Is it possible
To spy it in an eye,
That turns as soft as chance on die,
The truth whereof can any try,
    Is it possible?

It is possible
For to turn so oft,
To bring that lowest that was most aloft;
And to fall highest yet to light soft.
    It is possible.

All is possible,
Whoso list believe;
Trust therefore first and after preve:
As men wed ladies by licence and leave,
    All is possible.

SIR THOMAS WYATT

The Lover Showeth How He
Is Forsaken of Such
as He Sometime Enjoyed

They flee from me that sometime did me seek,
 With naked foot stalking in my chamber.
I have seen them gentle, tame and meek,
 That now are wild and do not remember
 That sometime they put themselves in danger
  To take bread at my hand; and now they range
  Busily seeking with a continual change.

Thankt be fortune, it hath been otherwise
 Twenty times better; but once, in special,
In thin array, after a pleasant guise,
 When her loose gown from her shoulders did fall,
 And she me caught in her arms long and small,
  Therewith all sweetly did me kiss,
  And softly said: "Dear heart, how like you this?"

It was no dream; I lay broad waking:
 But all is turned thorough my gentleness
Into a strange fashion of forsaking;
 And I have leave to go of her goodness;
 And she also to use new-fangleness.
  But since that I so kindely am served,
  I fain would know what she hath deserved.

SIR THOMAS WYATT

Complaint of the Absence of Her Lover
Being upon the Sea

O happy dames! that may embrace
 The fruit of your delight,
Help to bewail the woeful case
 And eke the heavy plight
Of me, that wonted to rejoice
The fortune of my pleasant choice:
Good ladies, help to fill my mourning voice.

In ship, freight with rememberance
  Of thoughts and pleasures past,
He sails that hath in governance
  My life while it will last:
With scalding sighs, for lack of gale,
Furthering his hope, that is his sail,
Toward me, the sweet port of his avail.

Alas! how oft in dreams I see
  Those eyes that were my food;
Which sometime so delighted me,
  That yet they do me good:
Wherewith I wake with his return,
Whose absent flame did make me burn:
But when I find the lack, Lord, how I mourn!

When other lovers in arms across
  Rejoice their chief delight,
Drownèd in tears, to mourn my loss
  I stand the bitter night
In my window, where I may see
Before the winds how the clouds flee:
Lo! what a mariner love hath made me!

And in green waves when the salt flood
  Doth rise by rage of wind,
A thousand fancies in that mood
  Assail my restless mind:
Alas! now drencheth my sweet foe,
That with the spoil of my heart did go,
And left me; but, alas! why did he so?

And when the seas wax calm again
  To chase fro me annoy,
My doubtful hope doth cause me plain:
  So dread cuts off my joy.
Thus is my wealth mingled with woe,
And of each thought a doubt doth grow;
Now he comes! Will he come? Alas, no, no!

HENRY HOWARD, EARL OF SURREY

cause me plain = make me lament

"His being was in her alone"

His being was in her alone:
And he not being, she was none.

They joyed one joy, one grief they grieved;
One love they loved, one life they lived.
The hand was one, one was the sword,
That did his death, her death afford.

As all the rest, so now the stone
That tombs the two is justly one.

SIR PHILIP SIDNEY

A Description of Love

Now what is love, I pray thee tell?
It is that fountain and that well
Where pleasure and repentance dwell.
It is perhaps that sauncing bell
That tolls all into heaven or hell:
And this is love, as I hear tell.

Yet what is love, I pray thee say?
It is a work on holy day.
It is December matched with May,
When lusty bloods in fresh array
Hear ten months after of the play:
And this is love, as I hear say.

Yet what is love, I pray thee sain?
It is a sunshine mixed with rain.
It is a tooth-ache, or like pain;
It is a game where none doth gain;
The lass saith No, and would full fain:
And this is love, as I hear sain.

Yet what is love, I pray thee say?
It is a yea, it is a nay,
A pretty kind of sporting fray;

It is a thing will soon away;
Then take the vantage while you may:
And this is love, as I hear say.

Yet what is love, I pray thee show?
A thing that creeps, it cannot go;
A prize that passeth to and fro;
A thing for one, a thing for mo;
And he that proves must find it so:
And this is love, sweet friend, I trow.

Sir Walter Ralegh

sauncing = sanctus

"What thing is love?"

What thing is love? for, well I wot, love is a thing.
It is a prick, it is a sting,
It is a pretty pretty thing;
It is a fire, it is a coal,
Whose flame creeps in at every hole;
And as my wit doth best devise,
Love's dwelling is in ladies' eyes:
From whence do glance love's piercing darts
That make such holes into our hearts;
And all the world herein accord
Love is a great and mighty lord,
And when he list to mount so high,
With Venus he in heaven doth lie,
And evermore hath been a god
Since Mars and she played even and odd.

George Peele

Sephestia's Song to Her Child

Weep not, my wanton, smile upon my knee;
When thou art old there's grief enough for thee.
  Mother's wag, pretty boy,
  Father's sorrow, father's joy;

When thy father first did see
Such a boy by him and me,
He was glad, I was woe;
Fortune changèd made him so,
When he left his pretty boy,
Last his sorrow, first his joy.

Weep not, my wanton, smile upon my knee;
When thou art old there's grief enough for thee.
  Streaming tears that never stint,
  Like pearl-drops from a flint,
  Fell by course from his eyes,
  That one another's place supplies;
  Thus he grieved in every part,
  Tears of blood fell from his heart,
  When he left his pretty boy,
  Father's sorrow, father's joy.

Weep not, my wanton, smile upon my knee;
When thou art old there's grief enough for thee.
  The wanton smiled, father wept,
  Mother cried, baby leapt;
  More he crowed, more we cried,
  Nature could not sorrow hide:
  He must go, he must kiss
  Child and mother, baby bliss,
  For he left his pretty boy,
  Father's sorrow, father's joy.
Weep not, my wanton, smile upon my knee;
When thou art old there's grief enough for thee.

ROBERT GREENE

Pan's Syrinx

Pan's Syrinx was a girl indeed,
Though now she's turned into a reed;
From that dear reed Pan's pipe does come,
A pipe that strikes Apollo dumb;
Nor flute, nor lute, nor gittern can
So chant it as the pipe of Pan:

Cross-gartered swains and dairy girls,
With faces smug and round as pearls,
When Pan's shrill pipe begins to play,
With dancing wear out night and day:
The bagpipe's drone his hum lays by
When Pan sounds up his minstrelsy;
His minstrelsy! oh, base! this quill—
Which at my mouth with wind I fill—
Puts me in mind, though her I miss,
That still my Syrinx' lips I kiss.

JOHN LYLY

The Passionate Shepherd to His Love

Come live with me, and be my love,
And we will all the pleasures prove,
That valleys, groves, hills and fields,
Woods, or steepy mountains yields.

And we will sit upon the rocks,
Seeing the shepherds feed their flocks,
By shallow rivers, to whose falls,
Melodious birds sing madrigals.

And I will make thee beds of roses,
And a thousand fragrant posies,
A cap of flowers, and a kirtle
Embroidered all with leaves of myrtle;

A gown made of the finest wool,
Which from our pretty lambs we pull,
Fair-linèd slippers for the cold,
With buckles of the purest gold;

A belt of straw and ivy buds
With coral clasps and amber studs:
And if these pleasures may thee move,
Come live with me, and be my love.

The shepherd swains shall dance and sing,
For thy delight each May morning:
If these delights thy mind may move,
Then live with me, and be my love.

CHRISTOPHER MARLOWE

Pastoral

Who can live in heart so glad
As the merry country lad?
Who upon a fair green balk
May at pleasure sit and walk,
And amid the azure skies
See the morning sun arise,
While he hears in every spring
How the birds do chirp and sing:
Or before the hounds in cry
See the hare go stealing by:
Or along the shallow brook,
Angling with a baited hook,
See the fishes leap and play
In a blessèd sunny day:
Or to hear the partridge call
Till she have her covey all:
Or to see the subtle fox,
How the villain plies the box;
After feeding on his prey,
How he closely sneaks away,
Through the hedge and down the furrow
Till he gets into his burrow:
Then the bees to gather honey;
And the little black-haired coney,
On a bank for sunny place,
With her forefeet wash her face,—
Are not these, with thousands more
Than the courts of kings do know,
The true pleasing spirit's sights
That may breed true love's delights?

NICHOLAS BRETON

balk = strip of unploughed ground
plies the box = seeks a way into the poultry-yard

"*Shine out, fair Sun*"

Shine out, fair Sun, with all your heat,
   Show all your thousand-coloured light!
Black Winter freezes to his seat;
   The grey wolf howls, he does so bite;
Crookt Age on three knees creeps the street;
   The boneless fish close quaking lies
And eats for cold his aching feet;
   The stars in icicles arise:
Shine out, and make this winter night
Our beauty's Spring, our Prince of Light!

ANON.

"*Enjoy thy April now*"

Enjoy thy April now,
Whilst it doth freely shine;
This lightning flash and show,
With that clear spirit of thine,
Will suddenly decline;
   And thou, fair murdering eyes,
Shall be Love's tombs, where now his cradle lies.

Thy gold and scarlet shall
Pale silver colour be;
Thy row of pearls shall fall
Like withered leaves from tree;
And thou shall shortly see
Thy face and hair to grow
All ploughed with furrows, over-swoln with snow.

That which on Flora's breast,
All fresh and flourishing,
Aurora, newly dressed,
Saw in her dawning spring;
Quite dry and languishing,
Deprived of honour quite,
Day-closing Hesperus beholds at night.

Fair is the lily, fair
The rose, of flowers the eye;
Both wither in the air,
Their beauteous colours die:
And so at length shall lie
Deprived of former grace,
The lilies of thy breasts, the roses of thy face.

What then will it avail,
O youth, advisèd ill,
In lap of Beauty frail
To nurse a wayward will,
Like snake in sun-warm hill?
Pluck, pluck betime thy flower,
That springs and parcheth in one short hour!

SAMUEL DANIEL

"I pray thee leave"

I pray thee leave, love me no more,
 Call home the heart you gave me!
I but in vain that saint adore
 That can but will not save me.
These poor half-kisses kill me quite;
 Was ever man thus servèd,
Amidst an ocean of delight,
 For pleasure to be stervèd?

Show me no more those snowy breasts
 With azure riverets branchèd,
Where, whilst mine eye with plenty feasts,
 Yet is my thirst not stanchèd.
O Tantalus, thy pains ne'er tell!
 By me thou art prevented:
'Tis nothing to be plagued in Hell,
 But thus in Heaven tormented!

Clip me no more in those dear arms,
 Nor thy life's comfort call me!
Oh, these are but too powerful charms,

And do but more enthral me.
But see, how patient I am grown
 In all this coil about thee!
Come, nice thing, let thy heart alone!
 I cannot live without thee.

MICHAEL DRAYTON

Upon the Sudden Restraint
of the Earl of Somerset,
Falling from Favour

Dazzled thus with height of place,
 Whilst our hopes our wits beguile,
No man marks the narrow space
 'Twixt a prison and a smile.

Then, since fortune's favours fade,
 You that in her arms do sleep,
Learn to swim, and not to wade;
 For the hearts of kings are deep.

But if greatness be so blind
 As to trust in towers of air,
Let it be with goodness lined,
 That at least the fall be fair.

Then, though darkened, you shall say,
 When friends fail and princes frown,
Virtue is the roughest way,
 But proves at night a bed of down.

SIR HENRY WOTTON

"Haymakers, rakers"

Haymakers, rakers, reapers, and mowers,
 Wait on your Summer-queen;
Dress up with musk-rose her eglantine bowers,
 Daffodils strew the green;

Sing, dance, and play,
'Tis holiday;
The sun does bravely shine
On our ears of corn.
Rich as a pearl
Comes every girl,
This is mine, this is mine, this is mine;
Let us die, ere away they be borne.

Bow to the Sun, to our queen, and that fair one
Come to behold our sports:
Each bonny lass here is counted a rare one,
As those in a prince's courts.
These and we
With country glee,
Will teach the woods to resound,
And the hills with echoes hollow:
Skipping lambs
Their bleating dams,
'Mongst kids shall trip it round;
For joy thus our wenches we follow.

Wind, jolly huntsmen, your neat bugles shrilly,
Hounds make a lusty cry;
Spring up, you falconers, the partridges freely,
Then let your brave hawks fly.
Horses amain,
Over ridge, over plain,
The dogs have the stag in chase:
'Tis a sport to content a king.
So ho ho! through the skies
How the proud bird flies,
And sousing kills with a grace!
Now the deer falls; hark, how they ring!

THOMAS DEKKER

sousing = swooping

"*Now winter nights*"

Now winter nights enlarge
The number of their hours,
And clouds their storms discharge

Upon the airy towers.
Let now the chimneys blaze,
And cups o'erflow with wine;
Let well-tuned words amaze
With harmony divine.
Now yellow waxen lights
Shall wait on honey love,
While youthful revels, masques, and courtly sights
Sleep's leaden spells remove.

This time doth well dispense
With lovers' long discourse;
Much speech hath some defence
Though beauty no remorse.
All do not all things well;
Some measures comely tread,
Some knotted riddles tell,
Some poems smoothly read.
The summer hath his joys
And winter his delights;
Though love and all his pleasures are but toys,
They shorten tedious nights.

THOMAS CAMPION

"Though I am young"

Though I am young and cannot tell
Either what Death or Love is well,
Yet I have heard they both bear darts,
And both do aim at human hearts;
And then again, I have been told,
Love wounds with heat, as Death with cold;
So that I fear they do but bring
Extremes to touch, and mean one thing.
As in a ruin we it call
One thing to be blown up, or fall;
Or to our end like way may have
By a flash of lightning, or a wave:
So Love's inflamèd shaft or brand,

May kill as soon as Death's cold hand;
Except Love's fires the virtue have
To fright the frost out of the grave.

                              BEN JONSON

Epitaph on Elizabeth, L.H.

Wouldst thou hear what man can say
In a little? Reader, stay.
Underneath this stone doth lie
As much beauty as could die;
Which in life did harbour give
To more virtue than doth live.
If at all she had a fault,
Leave it buried in this vault.
One name was Elizabeth,
Th' other, let it sleep with death:
Fitter, where it died, to tell
Than that it lived at all. Farewell.

                              BEN JONSON

Song

Sweetest Love, I do not go
    For weariness of thee,
Nor in hope the world can show
    A fitter love for me;
        But since that I
Must die at last, 'tis best
To use myself in jest
    Thus by feigned deaths to die.

Yesternight the sun went hence,
    And yet is here today;
He hath no desire nor sense,
    Nor half so short a way:
        Then fear not me,
But believe that I shall make

Speedier journeys, since I take
  More wings and spurs than he.

Oh, how feeble is man's power,
  That, if good fortune fall,
Cannot add another hour,
  Nor a lost hour recall!
    But come bad chance,
And we join it to our strength,
And we teach it art and length,
  Itself o'er us to advance.

When thou sigh'st, thou sigh'st not wind,
  But sigh'st my soul away;
When thou weep'st, unkindly kind,
  My life's blood doth decay.
    It cannot be
That thou lov'st me as thou say'st,
If in thine my life thou waste,
  Thou art the best of me.

Let not thy divining heart
  Forethink me any ill;
Destiny may take thy part,
  And may thy fears fulfil.
    But think that we
Are but turned aside to sleep:
They who one another keep
  Alive, ne'er parted be.

                              JOHN DONNE

Song

Go and catch a falling star;
  Get with child a mandrake root;
Tell me where all past years are,
  Or who cleft the Devil's foot;
Teach me to hear mermaids singing,
Or to keep off envy's stinging.

And find
What wind
Serves to advance an honest mind.

If thou be'st born to strange sights,
    Things invisible to see,
Ride ten thousand days and nights
    Till age snow white hairs on thee;
Thou, when thou return'st, wilt tell me ·
All strange wonders that befell thee,
            And swear
            No where
Lives a woman true and fair.

If thou find'st one, let me know;
    Such a pilgrimage were sweet.
Yet do not; I would not go,
    Though at next door we might meet.
Though she were true when you met her,
And last till you write your letter,
            Yet she
            Will be
False, ere I come, to two or three.

                          JOHN DONNE

"All the flowers of the spring"

All the flowers of the spring
Meet to perfume our burying;
These have but their growing prime,
And man doth flourish but his time:
Survey our progress from our birth;
We are set, we grow, we turn to earth.
Courts adieu, and all delights,
All bewitching appetites!
Sweetest breath and clearest eye,
Like perfumes, go out and die;
And consequently this is done
As shadows wait upon the sun.
Vain the ambition of kings

Who seek by trophies and dead things
To leave a living name behind,
And weave but nets to catch the wind.

JOHN WEBSTER

Madrigal

Like the Idalian queen,
Her hair about her eyne,
With neck and breast's ripe apples to be seen,
At first glance of the morn
In Cyprus' gardens gathering those fair flowers
Which of her blood were born,
I saw, but fainting saw, my paramours.
The Graces naked danced about the place,
The winds and trees amazed
With silence on her gazed,
The flowers did smile, like those upon her face;
And as their aspen stalks those fingers band,
That she might read my case,
A hyacinth I wished me in her hand.

WILLIAM DRUMMOND

"The ivory, coral, gold"

The ivory, coral, gold,
Of breast, of lips, of hair,
So lively Sleep doth show to inward sight,
That, wake, I think I hold
No shadow, but my fair:
Myself so to deceive,
With long-shut eyes I shun the irksome light.
Such pleasure thus I have,
Delighting in false gleams,
If Death Sleep's brother be,
And souls relieved of sense have so sweet dreams,
That I would wish me thus to dream and die.

WILLIAM DRUMMOND

In Commendation of Music

When whispering strains do softly steal
With creeping passion through the heart,
And when at every touch we feel
Our pulses beat and bear a part;
      When threads can make
      A heartstring shake,
      Philosophy
      Can scarce deny
The soul consists of harmony.

When unto heav'nly joy we feign
Whate'er the soul affecteth most,
Which only thus we can explain
By music of the wingèd host,
      Whose lays we think
      Make stars to wink,
      Philosophy
      Can scarce deny
Our souls consist of harmony.

O lull me, lull me, charming air,
My senses rock with wonder sweet;
Like snow on wool thy fallings are,
Soft, like a spirit's, are thy feet:
      Grief who need fear
      That hath an ear?
      Down let him lie
      And slumb'ring die,
And change his soul for harmony.

WILLIAM STRODE

On Chloris Walking in the Snow

I saw fair Chloris walk alone,
Whilst feathered rain came softly down,
And Jove descended from his tower
To court her in a silver shower.
The wanton snow flew on her breast

Like little birds unto their nest;
But overcome with whiteness there,
For grief it thawed into a tear;
Thence falling on her garment's hem,
To deck her, froze into a gem.

                                    WILLIAM STRODE

"Ask me no more"

Ask me no more where Jove bestows,
When June is past, the fading rose;
For in your beauties, orient deep,
These flowers, as in their causes, sleep.

Ask me no more whither do stray
The golden atoms of the day;
For in pure love heaven did prepare
Those powders to enrich your hair.

Ask me no more whither doth haste
The nightingale, when May is past;
For in your sweet dividing throat
She winters, and keeps warm her note.

Ask me no more where those stars light,
That downwards fall in dead of night;
For in your eyes they sit, and there
Fixèd become, as in their sphere.

Ask me no more if east or west
The phœnix builds her spicy nest;
For unto you at last she flies,
And in your fragrant bosom dies.

                                    THOMAS CAREW

"Under the willow shades"

Under the willow shades they were
  Free from the eye-sight of the sun,
For no intruding beam could there

Peep through to spy what things were done:
  Thus shelter'd, they unseen did lie,
  Surfeiting on each other's eye;
Defended by the willow shades alone,
The sun's heat they defied, and cool'd their own.

Whilst they did embrace unspied,
  The conscious willows seem'd to smile,
That they with privacy supplied,
  Holding the door, as 'twere, the while,
    And, when their dalliances were o'er,
    The willows, to oblige 'em more,
Bowing, did seem to say, as they withdrew,
We can supply you with a cradle, too.

SIR WILLIAM DAVENANT

To His Coy Mistress

Had we but world enough, and time,
This coyness, Lady, were no crime.
We would sit down, and think which way
To walk, and pass our long love's day.
Thou by the Indian Ganges' side
Shouldst rubies find; I by the tide
Of Humber would complain. I would
Love you ten years before the Flood;
And you should, if you please, refuse
Till the Conversion of the Jews.
My vegetable love should grow
Vaster than empires, and more slow.
An hundred years should go to praise
Thine eyes, and on thy forehead gaze;
Two hundred to adore each breast;
But thirty thousand to the rest:
An age, at least, to every part,
And the last age should show your heart.
For, Lady, you deserve this state;
Nor would I love at lower rate.
  But, at my back, I always hear
Time's wingèd chariot hurrying near:

And yonder, all before us lie
Deserts of vast eternity.
Thy beauty shall no more be found;
Nor, in thy marble vault, shall sound
My echoing song. Then worms shall try
That long-preserved virginity:
And your quaint honour turn to dust;
And into ashes all my lust.
The grave's a fine and private place,
But none, I think, do there embrace.
   Now, therefore, while the youthful hue
Sits on thy skin like morning dew,
And while thy willing soul transpires
At every pore with instant fires,
Now let us sport us while we may;
And now, like amorous birds of prey,
Rather at once our time devour,
Than languish in his slow-chapt power.
Let us roll all our strength, and all
Our sweetness, up into one ball;
And tear our pleasures, with rough strife,
Thorough the iron gates of life.
   Thus, though we cannot make our sun
Stand still, yet we will make him run.

ANDREW MARVELL

The Mower to the Glow-Worms

Ye living lamps, by whose dear light
   The nightingale does sit so late,
And, studying all the summer night,
   Her matchless songs does meditate;

Ye country comets, that portend
   No war, nor prince's funeral,
Shining unto no higher end
   Than to presage the grasses' fall;

Ye glow-worms, whose officious flame
   To wandering mowers shows the way,

That in the night have lost their aim,
    And after foolish fires do stray;

Your courteous lights in vain you waste,
    Since Juliana here is come;
For she my mind hath so displaced
    That I shall never find my home.

ANDREW MARVELL

Sic Vita

Like to the falling of a star;
Or as the flights of eagles are;
Or like the fresh Spring's gaudy hue;
Or silver drops of morning dew;
Or like a wind that chafes the flood;
Or bubbles which on water stood;
Even such is man, whose borrow'd light
Is straight call'd in, and paid to night.

    The wind blows out; the bubble dies;
    The Spring entomb'd in Autumn lies;
    The dew dries up; the star is shot;
    The flight is past; and man forgot.

HENRY KING

"Gaze not on swans"

Gaze not on swans, in whose soft breast
A full-hatched beauty seems to nest;
Nor snow, which falling from the sky
Hovers in its virginity.

Gaze not on roses, though new blown,
Graced with a fresh complexion;
Nor lilies, which no subtle bee
Hath robbed by kissing chymistry.

Gaze not on that pure milky way,
Where night vies splendour with the day;
Nor pearl, whose silver walls confine
The riches of an Indian mine.

For if my Emperess appears,
Swans moulting die, snow melts to tears,
Roses do blush and hang their heads,
Pale lilies shrink into their beds:

The milky way rides post to shroud
Its baffled glory in a cloud;
And pearls do climb into her ear,
To hang themselves for envy there.

So have I seen stars big with light
Prove lanthorns to the moon-eyed night,
Which when Sol's rays were once displayed,
Sunk in their sockets, and decayed.

HENRY NOEL

"Nymphs and shepherds"

Nymphs and shepherds, dance no more
     By sandy Ladon's lilied banks;
On old Lycæus or Cyllene hoar,
     Trip no more in twilight ranks;
Though Erymanth your loss deplore,
     A better soil shall give ye thanks.
From the stony Mænalus
Bring your flocks and live with us;
Here ye shall have greater grace,
To serve the Lady of this place.
Though Syrinx your Pan's mistress were,
Yet Syrinx well might wait on her.
     Such a rural queen
     All Arcadia hath not seen.

JOHN MILTON

"*Sabrina fair*"

Sabrina fair,
 Listen where thou art sitting
Under the glassy, cool, translucent wave,
 In twisted braids of lilies knitting
The loose train of thy amber-dropping hair;
 Listen for dear honour's sake,
 Goddess of the silver lake,
    Listen and save!

 Listen and appear to us,
 In name of great Oceanus,
 By the earth-shaking Neptune's mace,
 And Tethys' grave majestic pace;
 By hoary Nereus' wrinkled look,
 And the Carpathian wizard's hook;
 By scaly Triton's winding shell,
 And old soothsaying Glaucus' spell;
 By Leucothea's lovely hands,
 And her son that rules the strands;
 By Thetis' tinsel-slippered feet,
 And the songs of Sirens sweet;
 By dead Parthenope's dear tomb,
 And fair Ligea's golden comb,
 Wherewith she sits on diamond rocks
 Sleeking her soft alluring locks;
 By all the nymphs that nightly dance
 Upon thy streams with wily glance,—
 Rise, rise, and heave thy rosy head
 From thy coral-paven bed,
 And bridle in thy headlong wave,
 Till thou our summons answered have.
    Listen and save!

        JOHN MILTON

"*Sweet Echo, sweetest nymph*"

Sweet Echo, sweetest nymph that liv'st unseen
 Within thy airy shell
By slow Meander's margent green,

And in the violet-embroidered vale
    Where the love-lorn nightingale
Nightly to thee her sad song mourneth well;
Canst thou not tell me of a gentle pair
    That likest thy Narcissus are?
        Oh, if thou have
    Hid them in some flowery cave,
       Tell me but where,
Sweet queen of parley, daughter of the sphere!
So may'st thou be translated to the skies,
And give resounding grace to all heaven's harmonies.

JOHN MILTON

Sonnet

Dost see how unregarded now
    That piece of beauty passes?
There was a time when I did vow
    To that alone;
    But mark the fate of faces:
The red and white works now no more in me
Than if it could not charm, or I not see.

And yet the face continues good,
    And I have still desires,
Am still the selfsame flesh and blood,
    As apt to meet
    And suffer from those fires;
O! Some kind power unriddle where it lies,
Whether my heart be faulty, or her eyes?

She every day her man does kill,
    And I as often die;
Neither her power, then, nor my will
    Can question'd be,
    What is the mystery?
Sure Beauty's empires, like to greater states,
Have certain periods set, and hidden fates.

SIR JOHN SUCKLING

An Epitaph upon a Young Married Couple Dead and Buried Together

To these, whom Death again did wed,
This grave's their second marriage-bed;
For though the hand of Fate could force
'Twixt soul and body a divorce,
It could not sunder man and wife,
Because they both lived but one life.
Peace, good Reader, do not weep.
Peace, the lovers are asleep.
They, sweet turtles, folded lie
In the last knot Love could tie.
And though they lie as they were dead,
Their pillow stone, their sheets of lead,
(Pillow hard, and sheets not warm)
Love made the bed; they'll take no harm.
Let them sleep: let them sleep on,
Till this stormy night be gone,
Till the eternal morrow dawn;
Then the curtains will be drawn
And they wake into a light,
Whose day shall never die in night.

RICHARD CRASHAW

To Lucasta, Going to the Wars

Tell me not, Sweet, I am unkind,
    That from the nunnery
Of thy chaste breast, and quiet mind,
    To war and arms I fly.

True; a new mistress now I chase,
    The first foe in the field;
And with a stronger faith embrace
    A sword, a horse, a shield.

Yet this inconstancy is such,
    As you too shall adore;
I could not love thee, Dear, so much,
    Loved I not honour more.

RICHARD LOVELACE

"*Why should you swear?*"

Why should you swear I am forsworn,
Since thine I vowed to be?
Lady, it is already morn,
And 'twas last night I swore to thee
That fond impossibility.

Have I not loved thee much and long,
A tedious twelve hours' space?
I must all other beauties wrong,
And rob thee of a new embrace,
Could I still dote upon thy face.

Not but all joy in thy brown hair
By others may be found:
But I must search the black and fair,
Like skilful mineralists that sound
For treasure in unploughed-up ground.

Then if, when I have loved my round,
Thou prov'st the pleasant she,
With spoils of meaner beauties crowned
I laden will return to thee,
Ev'n sated with variety.

RICHARD LOVELACE

"*My cabinets are oyster-shells*"

My cabinets are oyster-shells,
In which I keep my orient pearls;
To open them I use the tide,
As keys to locks, which opens wide
The oyster shells, then out I take
Those orient pearls, and crowns do make;
And modest coral I do wear,
Which blushes when it touches air.
On silver waves I sit and sing,
And then the fish lie listening:
Then sitting on a rocky stone

I comb my hair with fishes' bone;
The whilst Apollo with his beams
Doth dry my hair from watery streams.
His light doth glaze the water's face,
Make the large sea my looking-glass:
So when I swim on waters high,
I see myself as I glide by:
But when the sun begins to burn,
I back into my waters turn,
And dive unto the bottom low:
Then on my head the waters flow
In curlèd waves and circles round,
And thus with waters am I crowned.

MARGARET CAVENDISH,
DUCHESS OF NEWCASTLE

Laura Sleeping

Winds, whisper gently whilst she sleeps,
  And fan her with your cooling wings;
Whilst she her drops of beauty weeps
  From pure and yet-unrivalled springs.

Glide over beauty's field, her face,
  To kiss her lip and cheek be bold,
But with a calm and stealing pace,
  Neither too rude, nor yet too cold.

Play in her beams, and crisp her hair,
  With such a gale as wings soft love,
And with so sweet, so rich an air,
  As breathes from the Arabian grove.

A breath as hushed as lover's sigh,
  Or that unfolds the morning door;
Sweet as the winds that gently fly
  To sweep the spring's enamelled floor.

Murmur soft music to her dreams,
  That pure and unpolluted run

Like to the new-born crystal streams
    Under the bright enamoured sun.

But when she waking shall display
    Her light, retire within your bar:
Her breath is life, her eyes are day,
    And all mankind her creatures are.

CHARLES COTTON

"Get you gone"

Get you gone, you will undo me,
If you love me don't pursue me;
Let that inclination perish
Which I dare no longer cherish.
With harmless thoughts I did begin,
But in the crowd love entered in;
I knew him not, he was so gay,
So innocent and full of play.
At every hour, in every place,
I either saw or form'd your face;
All that in plays was finely writ
Fancy for you and me did fit;
My dreams at night were all of you,
Such as till then I never knew.
I sported thus with young desire,
Never intending to go higher;
But now his teeth and claws are grown,
Let me the fatal lion shun.
You found me harmless; leave me so;
For, were I not, you'd leave me too.

SIR CHARLES SEDLEY

"Thus lovely sleep"

Thus lovely sleep did first appear,
    Ere yet it was with death allied,
When the first fair one, like her here,
    Lay down, and for a little died.

Ere happy souls knew how to die
　　And trod the rougher paths to bliss,
Transported in an ecstasy
　　　They breathed out such smooth ways as this.

Her hand bears gently up her head,
　　And like a pillow, raised does keep;
But softer than her couch is spread,
　　　Though that be softer than her sleep.

Alas! that death-like sleep or night
　　Should power have to close those eyes,
Which once vied with the fairest light
　　Or what gay colours thence did rise.

Ah! that lost beams thus long have shined
　　To them with darkness overspread,
Unseen as day breaks to the blind
　　Or the sun rises to the dead.

That sun in all his eastern pride
　　Did never see a shape so rare,
Nor night within its black arms hide
　　A silent beauty half so fair.

RICHARD LEIGH

A Better Answer

Dear Cloe, how blubbered is that pretty face?
　　Thy cheek all on fire, and thy hair all uncurled:
Prithee quit this caprice; and, as old Falstaff says,
　　Let us e'en talk a little like folks of this world.

How canst thou presume, thou hast leave to destroy
　　The beauties, which Venus but lent to thy keeping?
Those locks were designed to inspire love and joy:
　　More ordinary eyes may serve people for weeping.

To be vexed at a trifle or two that I writ,
   Your judgment at once, and my passion you wrong:
You take that for fact, which will scarce be found wit:
   Od's life! must one swear to the truth of a song?

What I speak, my fair Cloe, and what I write, shows
   The difference there is betwixt nature and art:
I court others in verse; but I love thee in prose:
   And they have my whimsies; but thou hast my heart.

The god of us verse-men, you know child, the sun,
   How after his journeys he sets up his rest:
If at morning o'er earth 'tis his fancy to run;
   At night he reclines on his Thetis's breast.

So when I am wearied with wandering all day;
   To thee my delight in the evening I come:
No matter what beauties I saw in my way:
   They were but my visits; but thou art my home.

Then finish, dear Cloe, this pastoral war;
   And let us like Horace and Lydia agree:
For thou art a girl as much brighter than her,
   As he was a poet sublimer than me.

MATTHEW PRIOR

The Despairing Lover

   Distracted with care,
   For Phillis the fair;
   Since nothing could move her,
   Poor Damon, her lover,
   Resolves in despair
   No longer to languish,
   Nor bear so much anguish;
   But, mad with his love,
   To a precipice goes;

Where a leap from above
Would soon finish his woes.

When in rage he came there,
Beholding how steep
The sides did appear,
And the bottom how deep;
His torments projecting,
And sadly reflecting,
That a lover forsaken
A new love may get;
But a neck, when once broken,
Can never be set:
And, that he could die
Whenever he would;
But, that he could live
But as long as he could:
How grievous soever
The torment might grow,
He scorn'd to endeavour
To finish it so.
But bold, unconcern'd
At thoughts of the pain,
He calmly return'd
To his cottage again.

WILLIAM WALSH

"Pious Celinda"

Pious Celinda goes to prayers,
    If I but ask the favour;
And yet the tender fool's in tears
    When she believes I'll leave her.

Would I were free from this restraint,
    Or else had hopes to win her;
Would she could make of me a saint,
    Or I of her a sinner.

WILLIAM CONGREVE

To Miss Charlotte Pulteney
in Her Mother's Arms

Timely blossom, infant fair,
Fondling of a happy pair,
Every morn, and every night,
Their solicitous delight,
Sleeping, waking, still at ease,
Pleasing, without skill to please,
Little gossip, blithe and hale,
Tatling many a broken tale,
Singing many a tuneless song,
Lavish of a heedless tongue,
Simple maiden, void of art,
Babbling out the very heart,
Yet abandon'd to thy will,
Yet imagining no ill,
Yet too innocent to blush,
Like the linlet in the bush,
To the Mother-linnet's note
Moduling her slender throat,
Chirping forth thy petty joys,
Wanton in the change of toys,
Like the linnet green, in May
Flitting to each bloomy spray,
Wearied then, and glad of rest,
Like the linlet in the nest.
This thy present happy lot,
This, in time, will be forgot:
Other pleasures, other cares,
Ever-busy Time prepares.
And thou shalt in thy daughter see,
This picture, once, resembled thee.

                              AMBROSE PHILIPS

A Short Song of Congratulation

Long-expected one and twenty,
Ling'ring year, at last is flown;
Pomp and pleasure, pride and plenty,
Great Sir John, are all your own.

Loosen'd from the minor's tether,
Free to mortgage or to sell,
Wild as wind, and light as feather,
Bid the slaves of thrift farewell.

Call the Bettys, Kates, and Jennys,
Every name that laughs at care,
Lavish of your grandsire's guineas,
Show the spirit of an heir.

All that prey on vice and folly
Joy to see their quarry fly,
Here the gamester light and jolly,
There the lender grave and sly.

Wealth, Sir John, was made to wander,
Let it wander as it will:
See the jockey, see the pander,
Bid them come, and take their fill.

When the bonny blade carouses,
Pockets full, and spirits high,
What are acres? What are houses?
Only dirt, or wet or dry.

If the guardian or the mother
Tell the woes of wilful waste,
Scorn their counsel and their pother,
You can hang or drown at last.

SAMUEL JOHNSON

Ode

How sleep the brave, who sink to rest,
By all their country's wishes bless'd!
When Spring, with dewy fingers cold,
Returns to deck their hallow'd mould,
She there shall dress a sweeter sod
Than Fancy's feet have ever trod.

By fairy hands their knell is rung;
By forms unseen their dirge is sung;
There Honour comes, a pilgrim gray,
To bless the turf that wraps their clay;
And Freedom shall a while repair,
To dwell a weeping hermit there!

WILLIAM COLLINS

Dirge in Cymbeline

To fair Fidele's grassy tomb
　Soft maids and village hinds shall bring
Each opening sweet of earliest bloom,
　And rifle all the breathing spring.

No wailing ghost shall dare appear
　To vex with shrieks this quiet grove:
But shepherd lads assemble here,
　And melting virgins own their love.

No wither'd witch shall here be seen:
　No goblins lead their nightly crew:
The female fays shall haunt the green,
　And dress thy grave with pearly dew!

The redbreast oft, at evening hours,
　Shall kindly lend his little aid,
With hoary moss, and gather'd flowers,
　To deck the ground where thou art laid.

When howling winds and beating rain,
　In tempests shake the sylvan cell;
Or 'midst the chase, on every plain,
　The tender thought on thee shall dwell;

Each lonely scene shall thee restore;
　For thee the tear be duly shed;
Beloved till life can charm no more,
　And mourn'd till Pity's self be dead.

WILLIAM COLLINS

Stanzas on Woman

When lovely woman stoops to folly,
  And finds too late that men betray,
What charm can sooth her melancholy,
  What art can wash her guilt away?

The only art her guilt to cover,
  To hide her shame from ev'ry eye,
To give repentance to her lover,
  And wring his bosom—is, to die.

OLIVER GOLDSMITH

The Poplar Field

The poplars are fell'd; farewell to the shade
And the whispering sound of the cool colonnade;
The winds play no longer and sing in the leaves,
Nor Ouse on his bosom their image receives.

Twelve years have elapsed since I first took a view
Of my favourite field, and the bank where they grew:
And now in the grass behold they are laid,
And the tree is my seat that once lent me a shade.

The blackbird has fled to another retreat,
Where the hazels afford him a screen from the heat;
And the scene where his melody charm'd me before
Resounds with his sweet-flowing ditty no more.

My fugitive years are all hasting away,
And I must ere long lie as lowly as they,
With a turf on my breast and a stone at my head,
Ere another such grove shall arise in its stead.

'Tis a sight to engage me, if anything can,
To muse on the perishing pleasures of man;
Though his life be a dream, his enjoyments, I see,
Have a being less durable even than he.

WILLIAM COWPER

"Hear the voice of the Bard!"

Hear the voice of the Bard!
Who Present, Past, and Future, sees;
Whose ears have heard
The Holy Word
That walk'd among the ancient trees,

Calling the lapsèd Soul,
And weeping in the evening dew;
That might control
The starry pole,
And fallen, fallen light renew!

"O Earth, O Earth, return!
Arise from out the dewy grass;
Night is worn,
And the morn
Rises from the slumberous mass.

"Turn away no more;
Why wilt thou turn away?
The starry floor,
The wat'ry shore,
Is giv'n thee till the break of day."

WILLIAM BLAKE

"O Rose, thou art sick!"

O Rose, thou art sick!
The invisible worm,
That flies in the night,
In the howling storm,

Has found out thy bed
Of crimson joy;
And his dark secret love
Does thy life destroy.

WILLIAM BLAKE

"Ah, Sunflower"

Ah, Sunflower! weary of time,
Who countest the steps of the Sun;
Seeking after that sweet golden clime,
Where the traveller's journey is done;

Where the Youth pined away with desire,
And the pale Virgin shrouded in snow,
Arise from their graves, and aspire
Where my Sunflower wishes to go.

WILLIAM BLAKE

"Never seek to tell thy love"

Never seek to tell thy love,
Love that never told can be;
For the gentle wind does move
Silently, invisibly.

I told my love, I told my love,
I told her all my heart;
Trembling, cold, in ghastly fears,
Ah! she doth depart.

Soon as she was gone from me,
A traveller came by,
Silently, invisibly:
He took her with a sigh.

WILLIAM BLAKE

To the Cuckoo

O blithe New-comer! I have heard,
I hear thee and rejoice.
O Cuckoo! shall I call thee Bird,
Or but a wandering Voice?

While I am lying on the grass
Thy twofold shout I hear;

From hill to hill it seems to pass
At once far off, and near.

Though babbling only to the Vale,
Of sunshine and of flowers,
Thou bringest unto me a tale
Of visionary hours.

Thrice welcome, darling of the Spring!
Even yet thou art to me
No bird, but an invisible thing,
A voice, a mystery;

The same whom in my schoolboy days
I listened to; that Cry
Which made me look a thousand ways
In bush, and tree, and sky.

To seek thee did I often rove
Through woods and on the green;
And thou wert still a hope, a love;
Still longed for, never seen.

And I can listen to thee yet;
Can lie upon the plain
And listen, till I do beget
That golden time again.

O blessèd Bird! the earth we pace
Again appears to be
An unsubstantial, færy place;
That is fit home for Thee!

WILLIAM WORDSWORTH

"She dwelt among the untrodden ways"

She dwelt among the untrodden ways
    Beside the springs of Dove,
A Maid whom there were none to praise
    And very few to love:

A violet by a mossy stone
  Half hidden from the eye!
—Fair as a star, when only one
  Is shining in the sky.

She lived unknown, and few could know
  When Lucy ceased to be;
But she is in her grave, and, oh,
  The difference to me!

WILLIAM WORDSWORTH

"A slumber did my spirit seal"

A slumber did my spirit seal;
  I had no human fears:
She seemed a thing that could not feel
  The touch of earthly years.

No motion has she now, no force:
  She neither hears nor sees;
Rolled round in earth's diurnal course,
  With rocks, and stones, and trees.

WILLIAM WORDSWORTH

Kubla Khan

In Xanadu did Kubla Khan
A stately pleasure-dome decree:
Where Alph, the sacred river, ran
Through caverns measureless to man
  Down to a sunless sea.
So twice five miles of fertile ground
With walls and towers were girdled round:
And there were gardens bright with sinuous rills,
Where blossomed many an incense-bearing tree;
And here were forests ancient as the hills,
Enfolding sunny spots of greenery.

But oh! that deep romantic chasm which slanted
Down the green hill athwart a cedarn cover!
A savage place! as holy and enchanted
As e'er beneath a waning moon was haunted
By woman wailing for her demon-lover!
And from this chasm, with ceaseless turmoil seething,
As if this earth in fast thick pants were breathing,
A mighty fountain momently was forced:
Amid whose swift half-intermitted burst
Huge fragments vaulted like rebounding hail,
Or chaffy grain beneath the thresher's flail:
And 'mid these dancing rocks at once and ever
It flung up momently the sacred river.
Five miles meandering with a mazy motion
Through wood and dale the sacred river ran,
Then reached the caverns measureless to man,
And sank in tumult to a lifeless ocean:
And 'mid this tumult Kubla heard from far
Ancestral voices prophesying war!
   The shadow of the dome of pleasure
    Floated midway on the waves;
   Where was heard the mingled measure
    From the fountain and the caves.
It was a miracle of rare device,
A sunny pleasure-dome with caves of ice!

   A damsel with a dulcimer
   In a vision once I saw:
   It was an Abyssinian maid,
   And on her dulcimer she played,
   Singing of Mount Abora.
   Could I revive within me
    Her symphony and song,
   To such a deep delight 'twould win me,
    That with music loud and long,
   I would build that dome in air,
   That sunny dome! those caves of ice!
   And all who heard should see them there,
   And all should cry, Beware! Beware!
   His flashing eyes, his floating hair!
   Weave a circle round him thrice,

And close your eyes with holy dread,
For he on honey-dew hath fed,
And drunk the milk of Paradise.

SAMUEL TAYLOR COLERIDGE

On Ternissa's Death

Ternissa! you are fled!
I say not to the dead,
But to the happy ones who rest below:
For, surely, surely, where
Your voice and graces are,
Nothing of death can any feel or know.
Girls who delight to dwell
Where grows most asphodel,
Gather to their calm breasts each word you speak:
The mild Persephone
Places you on her knee,
And your cool palm smoothes down stern Pluto's cheek.

WALTER SAVAGE LANDOR

"Past ruin'd Ilion"

Past ruin'd Ilion Helen lives,
Alcestis rises from the shades;
Verse calls them forth; 'tis verse that gives
Immortal youth to mortal maids.

Soon shall Oblivion's deepening veil
Hide all the peopled hills you see,
The gay, the proud, while lovers hail
In distant ages you and me.

The tear for fading beauty check,
For passing glory cease to sigh;
One form shall rise above the wreck,
One name, Ianthe, shall not die.

WALTER SAVAGE LANDOR

Rose Aylmer

Ah what avails the sceptred race,
　　Ah what the form divine!
What every virtue, every grace!
　　Rose Aylmer, all were thine.
Rose Aylmer, whom these wakeful eyes
　　May weep, but never see,
A night of memories and of sighs
　　I consecrate to thee.

WALTER SAVAGE LANDOR

"She walks in beauty"

She walks in beauty, like the night
　　Of cloudless climes and starry skies;
And all that's best of dark and bright
　　Meet in her aspect and her eyes:
Thus mellow'd to that tender light
　　Which heaven to gaudy day denies.

One shade the more, one ray the less,
　　Had half impair'd the nameless grace
Which waves in every raven tress,
　　Or softly lightens o'er her face;
Where thoughts serenely sweet express
　　How pure, how dear their dwelling-place.

And on that cheek, and o'er that brow,
　　So soft, so calm, yet eloquent,
The smiles that win, the tints that glow,
　　But tell of days in goodness spent,
A mind at peace with all below,
　　A heart whose love is innocent!

GEORGE GORDON, LORD BYRON

"There be none of Beauty's daughters"

There be none of Beauty's daughters
 With a magic like thee;
And like music on the waters
 Is thy sweet voice to me:
When, as if its sound were causing
The charmèd ocean's pausing,
The waves lie still and gleaming,
And the lull'd winds seem dreaming:

And the midnight moon is weaving
 Her bright chain o'er the deep;
Whose breast is gently heaving,
 As an infant's asleep:
So the spirit bows before thee,
To listen and adore thee;
With a full but soft emotion,
Like the swell of Summer's ocean.

    GEORGE GORDON, LORD BYRON

To . . . . . .

One word is too often profaned
 For me to profane it,
One feeling too falsely disdained
 For thee to disdain it;
One hope is too like despair
 For prudence to smother,
And pity from thee more dear
 Than that from another.

I can give not what men call love,
 But wilt thou accept not
The worship the heart lifts above
 And the Heavens reject not,—
The desire of the moth for the star,
 Of the night for the morrow,
The devotion to something afar
 From the sphere of our sorrow?

    PERCY BYSSHE SHELLEY

"A widow bird sate mourning"

A widow bird sate mourning for her love
    Upon a wintry bough;
The frozen wind crept on above,
    The freezing stream below.

There was no leaf upon the forest bare,
    No flower upon the ground,
And little motion in the air
    Except the mill-wheel's sound.

           PERCY BYSSHE SHELLEY

"On a poet's lips I slept"

On a poet's lips I slept
Dreaming like a love-adept
In the sound his breathing kept;
Nor seeks nor finds he mortal blisses,
But feeds on the aëreal kisses
Of shapes that haunt thought's wildernesses.
He will watch from dawn to gloom
The lake-reflected sun illume
The yellow bees in the ivy-bloom,
Nor heed nor see, what things they be;
But from these create he can
Forms more real than living man,
Nurslings of immortality!
One of these awakened me,
And I sped to succour thee.

           PERCY BYSSHE SHELLEY

"I ne'er was struck"

I ne'er was struck before that hour
    With love so sudden and so sweet.
Her face it bloomed like a sweet flower
    And stole my heart away complete.

My face turned pale as deadly pale,
    My legs refused to walk away,
And when she looked "what could I ail?"
    My life and all seemed turned to clay.

And then my blood rushed to my face
    And took my sight away.
The trees and bushes round the place
    Seemed midnight at noonday.
I could not see a single thing,
    Words from my eyes did start;
They spoke as chords do from the string
    And blood burnt round my heart.

Are flowers the winter's choice?
    Is love's bed always snow?
She seemed to hear my silent voice
    And love's appeal to know.
I never saw so sweet a face
    As that I stood before:
My heart has left its dwelling-place
    And can return no more.

                JOHN CLARE

"Love, meet me in the green glen"

Love, meet me in the green glen,
    Beside the tall elm-tree,
Where the sweetbrier smells so sweet agen;
    There come with me,
        Meet me in the green glen.

Meet me at the sunset
    Down in the green glen,
Where we've often met
    By hawthorn-tree and foxes' den,
        Meet me in the green glen.

Meet me in the green glen,
    By sweetbrier bushes there;

Meet me by your own sen,
   Where the wild thyme blossoms fair.
   Meet me in the green glen.

Meet me by the sweetbrier,
   By the mole-hill swelling there;
When the west glows like a fire
   God's crimson bed is there.
   Meet me in the green glen.

JOHN CLARE

sen = self

"*I lost the love of heaven*"

I lost the love of heaven above,
   I spurned the lust of earth below,
I felt the sweets of fancied love,
   And hell itself my only foe.

I lost earth's joys, but felt the glow
   Of heaven's flame abound in me,
Till loveliness and I did grow
   The bard of immortality.

I loved, but woman fell away;
   I hid me from her faded flame.
I snatched the sun's eternal ray
   And wrote till earth was but a name.

In every language upon earth,
   On every shore, o'er every sea,
I gave my name immortal birth
   And kept my spirit with the free.

JOHN CLARE

"*In a drear-nighted December*"

In a drear-nighted December,
   Too happy, happy tree,
Thy branches ne'er remember

Their green felicity:
The north cannot undo them,
With a sleety whistle through them;
Nor frozen thawings glue them
From budding at the prime.

In a drear-nighted December,
Too happy, happy brook,
Thy bubblings ne'er remember
Apollo's summer look;
But with a sweet forgetting,
They stay their crystal fretting,
Never, never petting
About the frozen time.

Ah! would 'twere so with many
A gentle girl and boy!
But were there ever any
Writh'd not at passèd joy?
The feel of not to feel it,
When none there is to heal it,
Nor numbèd sense to steel it,
Was never said in rhyme.

JOHN KEATS

"We watch'd her breathing"

We watch'd her breathing thro' the night,
Her breathing soft and low,
As in her breast the wave of life
Kept heaving to and fro!

So silently we seemed to speak—
So slowly moved about!
As we had lent her half our powers
To eke her living out!

Our very hopes belied our fears
Our fears our hopes belied—

We thought her dying when she slept,
And sleeping when she died!

For when the morn came dim and sad—
And chill with early showers,
Her quiet eyelids closed—she had
Another morn than ours!

THOMAS HOOD

"I remember, I remember"

I remember, I remember,
The house where I was born,
The little window where the sun
Came peeping in at morn;
He never came a wink too soon,
Nor brought too long a day,
But now, I often wish the night
Had borne my breath away!

I remember, I remember,
The roses, red and white,
The violets, and the lily-cups,
Those flowers made of light!
The lilacs where the robin built,
And where my brother set
The laburnum on his birthday,—
The tree is living yet!

I remember, I remember,
Where I was used to swing,
And thought the air must rush as fresh
To swallows on the wing;
My spirit flew in feathers then,
That is so heavy now,
And summer pools could hardly cool
The fever on my brow!

I remember, I remember,
The fir trees dark and high;

I used to think their slender tops
Were close against the sky:
It was a childish ignorance,
But now 'tis little joy
To know I'm farther off fron heav'n
Than when I was a boy.

THOMAS HOOD

The Clote

O zummer clote! when the brook's a-sliden
  So slow an' smooth down his zedgy bed,
Upon thy broad leaves so seäfe a-riden
  The water's top wi' thy yoller head.
    By black rin'd allers,
    An' weedy shallers
Thee then dost float, goolden zummer clote!

The grey-bough'd withy's a-leänen lowly
  Above the water thy leaves do hide;
The benden bulrush, a-swaÿen slowly,
  Do skirt in zummer thy river's zide;
    An' perch in shoals, O,
    Do vill the holes, O,
Where thee dost float, goolden zummer clote!

Oh, when thy brook-drinken flow'r 's a-blowen,
  The burnen zummer's a-zetten in;
The time o' greenness, the time o' mowen,
  When in the haÿ-vield, wi' zunburnt skin,
    The vo'k do drink, O,
    Upon the brink, O,
Where thee dost float, goolden zummer clote!

Wi' eärms a-spreaden, an' cheäks a-blowen,
  How proud wer I when I vu'st could zwim
Athirt the deep pleäce where thou bist growen,
  Wi' thy long more vrom the bottom dim;
    While cows, knee-high, O,
    In brook, wer nigh, O,
Where thee dost float, goolden zummer clote!

Ov all the brooks drough the meäds a-winden,
  Ov all the meäds by a river's brim,
There's nwone so feäir o' my own heart's vinden,
  As where the maïdens do zee thee swim,
    An' stan' to teäke, O,
    Wi' long-stemm'd reäke, O,
Thy flow'r afloat, goolden zummer clote!

                          WILLIAM BARNES

clote = golden water-lily: *yoller* = yellow
aller = alder tree: *more* = stalk: *vinden* = finding

The Wife a-Lost

Since I noo mwore do zee your feäce,
  Up steäirs or down below,
I'll zit me in the lwonesome pleäce,
  Where flat-bough'd beech do grow:
Below the beeches' bough, my love,
  Where you did never come,
An' I don't look to meet ye now,
  As I do look at hwome.

Since you noo mwore be at my zide,
  In walks in zummer het,
I'll goo alwone where mist do ride,
  Drough trees a-drippen wet:
Below the raïn-wet bough, my love,
  Where you did never come,
An' I don't grieve to miss ye now,
  As I do grieve at hwome.

Since now bezide my dinner-bwoard
  Your vaïce do never sound,
I'll eat the bit I can avword,
  A-vield upon the ground;
Below the darksome bough, my love,
  Where you did never dine,

drough = through

An' I don't grieve to miss ye now,
  As I at hwome do pine.
Since I do miss your vaïce an' feäce
  In praÿer at eventide,
I'll praÿ wi' woone sad vaïce vor greäce
  To goo where you do bide;
Above the tree an' bough, my love,
  Where you be gone avore,
An' be a-waïten vor me now,
  To come vor evermwore.

WILLIAM BARNES

The Wind at the Door

As day did darken on the dewless grass
There still wi' nwone a-come by me,
To staÿ a-while at hwome by me;
Within the house, all dumb by me,
I zot me sad as the eventide did pass.

An' there a win'-blast shook the rattlen door,
An' seemed, as win' did mwone without,
As if my Jeäne, alwone without,
A-stannen on the stone without,
Wer there a-come wi' happiness oonce mwore.

I went to door; an' out vrom trees above
My head, upon the blast by me,
Sweet blossoms wer a-cast by me,
As if my love, a-past by me,
Did fling em down—a token ov her love.

"Sweet blossoms o' the tree where I do murn,"
I thought, "if you did blow vor her,
Vor apples that should grow vor her,
A-vallen down below vor her,
O then how happy I should zee you kern."

kern = to grow into fruit

But no. Too soon I voun' my charm abroke.
Noo comely soul in white like her—
Noo soul a-steppen light like her—
An' nwone o' comely height like her—
Went by; but all my grief ageän awoke.

WILLIAM BARNES

Old Adam

Old Adam, the carrion crow,
  The old crow of Cairo;
He sat in the shower, and let it flow
  Under his tail and over his crest;
    And through every feather
    Leaked the wet weather;
  And the bough swung under his nest;
For his beak it was heavy with marrow.
    Is that the wind dying? O no;
    It's only two devils, that blow
    Through a murderer's bones, to and fro,
      In the ghosts' moonshine.

Ho! Eve, my grey carrion wife,
  When we have supped on kings' marrow,
Where shall we drink and make merry our life?
  Our nest it is queen Cleopatra's skull,
    'Tis cloven and cracked,
    And battered and hacked,
  But with tears of blue eyes it is full:
Let us drink then, my raven of Cairo.
    Is that the wind dying? O no;
    It's only two devils, that blow
    Through a murderer's bones, to and fro,
      In the ghosts' moonshine.

THOMAS LOVELL BEDDOES

"We do lie beneath the grass"

We do lie beneath the grass
  In the moonlight, in the shade
Of the yew-tree. They that pass

Hear us not. We are afraid
    They would envy our delight,
    In our graves by glow-worm night.
Come follow us, and smile as we;
    We sail to the rock in the ancient waves,
Where the snow falls by thousands into the sea,
    And the drowned and the shipwrecked have
        happy graves.

THOMAS LOVELL BEDDOES

The Poet's Song

The rain had fallen, the Poet arose,
    He pass'd by the town and out of the street,
A light wind blew from the gates of the sun,
    And waves of shadow went over the wheat,
And he sat him down in a lonely place,
    And chanted a melody loud and sweet,
That made the wild-swan pause in her cloud,
    And the lark drop down at his feet.

The swallow stopt as he hunted the fly,
    The snake slipt under a spray,
The wild hawk stood with the down on his beak,
    And stared, with his foot on the prey,
And the nightingale thought, "I have sung many songs,
    But never a one so gay,
For he sings of what the world will be
    When the years have died away."

ALFRED, LORD TENNYSON

"The splendour falls"

The splendour falls on castle walls
    And snowy summits old in story;
The long light shakes across the lakes,
    And the wild cataract leaps in glory.
Blow, bugle, blow, set the wild echoes flying,
Blow, bugle; answer, echoes, dying, dying, dying.

O hark, O hear! how thin and clear,
    And thinner, clearer, farther going!
O sweet and far from cliff and scar
    The horns of Elfland faintly blowing!
Blow, let us hear the purple glens replying;
Blow, bugle; answer, echoes, dying, dying, dying.

O love, they die in yon rich sky,
    They faint on hill or field or river;
Our echoes roll from soul to soul,
    And grow for ever and for ever.
Blow, bugle, blow, set the wild echoes flying,
And answer, echoes, answer, dying, dying, dying.

ALFRED, LORD TENNYSON

"Tears, idle tears"

Tears, idle tears, I know not what they mean,
Tears from the depth of some divine despair
Rise in the heart, and gather to the eyes,
In looking on the happy Autumn fields,
And thinking of the days that are no more.

Fresh as the first beam glittering on a sail,
That brings our friends up from the underworld,
Sad as the last which reddens over one
That sinks with all we love below the verge;
So sad, so fresh, the days that are no more.

Ah, sad and strange as in dark summer dawns
The earliest pipe of half-awaken'd birds
To dying ears, when unto dying eyes
The casement slowly grows a glimmering square;
So sad, so strange, the days that are no more.

Dear as remember'd kisses after death,
And sweet as those by hopeless fancy feign'd
On lips that are for others; deep as love,
Deep as first love, and wild with all regret;
O Death in Life, the days that are no more.

ALFRED, LORD TENNYSON

from
In Memoriam

II

Old Yew, which graspest at the stones
    That name the under-lying dead,
    Thy fibres net the dreamless head,
Thy roots are wrapt about the bones.

The seasons bring the flower again,
    And bring the firstling to the flock;
    And in the dusk of thee, the clock
Beats out the little lives of men.

O not for thee the glow, the bloom,
    Who changest not in any gale,
    Nor branding summer suns avail
To touch thy thousand years of gloom:

And gazing on thee, sullen tree,
    Sick for thy stubborn hardihood,
    I seem to fail from out my blood
And grow incorporate into thee.

XI

Calm is the morn without a sound,
    Calm as to suit a calmer grief,
    And only thro' the faded leaf
The chestnut pattering to the ground:

Calm and deep peace on this high wold,
    And on these dews that drench the furze,
    And all the silvery gossamers
That twinkle into green and gold:

Calm and still light on yon great plain
    That sweeps with all its autumn bowers,
    And crowded farms and lessening towers,
To mingle with the bounding main:

Calm and deep peace in this wide air,
    These leaves that redden to the fall;
    And in my heart, if calm at all,
If any calm, a calm despair:

Calm on the seas, and silver sleep,
    And waves that sway themselves in rest,
    And dead calm in that noble breast
Which heaves but with the heaving deep.

CI

Unwatch'd, the garden bough shall sway,
    The tender blossom flutter down,
    Unloved, that beech will gather brown,
This maple burn itself away;

Unloved, the sun-flower, shining fair,
    Ray round with flames her disk of seed,
    And many a rose-carnation feed
With summer spice the humming air;

Unloved, by many a sandy bar,
    The brook shall babble down the plain,
    At noon or when the lesser wain
Is twisting round the polar star;

Uncared for, gird the windy grove,
    And flood the haunts of hern and crake;
    Or into silver arrows break
The sailing moon in creek and cove;

Till from the garden and the wild
    A fresh association blow,
    And year by year the landscape grow
Familiar to the stranger's child;

As year by year the labourer tills
    His wonted glebe, or lops the glades;
    And year by year our memory fades
From all the circle of the hills.

ALFRED, LORD TENNYSON

from
Maud

I

I have led her home, my love, my only friend.
There is none like her, none.
And never yet so warmly ran my blood
And sweetly, on and on
Calming itself to the long-wish'd-for end,
Full to the banks, close on the promised good.

II

None like her, none.
Just now the dry-tongued laurels' pattering talk
Seem'd her light foot along the garden walk,
And shook my heart to think she comes once more;
But even then I heard her close the door,
The gates of Heaven are closed, and she is gone.

III

There is none like her, none.
Nor will be when our summers have deceased.
O, art thou sighing for Lebanon
In the long breeze that streams to thy delicious East,
Sighing for Lebanon,
Dark cedar, tho' thy limbs have here increased,
Upon a pastoral slope as fair,
And looking to the South, and fed
With honey'd rain and delicate air,
And haunted by the starry head
Of her whose gentle will has changed my fate,
And made my life a perfumed altar-flame;
And over whom thy darkness must have spread
With such delight as theirs of old, thy great
Forefathers of the thornless garden, there
Shadowing the snow-limb'd Eve from whom she came.

ALFRED, LORD TENNYSON

Two in the Campagna

I wonder do you feel today
   As I have felt since, hand in hand,
We sat down on the grass, to stray
   In spirit better through the land,
This morn of Rome and May?

For me, I touched a thought, I know,
   Has tantalized me many times,
(Like turns of thread the spiders throw
   Mocking across our path) for rhymes
To catch at and let go.

Help me to hold it! First it left
   The yellowing fennel, run to seed
There, branching from the brickwork's cleft,
   Some old tomb's ruin: yonder weed
Took up the floating weft,

Where one small orange cup amassed
   Five beetles,—blind and green they grope
Among the honey-meal: and last,
   Everywhere on the grassy slope
I traced it. Hold it fast!

The champaign with its endless fleece
   Of feathery grasses everywhere!
Silence and passion, joy and peace,
   An everlasting wash of air—
Rome's ghost since her decease.

Such life here, through such length of hours,
   Such miracles performed in play,
Such primal naked forms of flowers,
   Such letting nature have her way
While heaven looks from its towers!

How say you? Let us, O my dove,
   Let us be unashamed of soul,
As earth lies bare to heaven above!

How is it under our control
To love or not to love?

I would that you were all to me,
    You that are just so much, no more.
Nor yours nor mine, nor slave nor free!
    Where does the fault lie? What the core
O' the wound, since wound must be?

I would I could adopt your will,
    See with your eyes, and set my heart
Beating by yours, and drink my fill
    At your soul's springs,—your part my part
In life, for good and ill.

No. I yearn upward, touch you close,
    Then stand away. I kiss your cheek,
Catch your soul's warmth,—I pluck the rose
    And love it more than tongue can speak—
Then the good minute goes.

Already how am I so far
    Out of that minute? Must I go
Still like the thistle-ball, no bar,
    Onward, whenever light winds blow,
Fixed by no friendly star?

Just when I seemed about to learn!
    Where is the thread now? Off again!
The old trick! Only I discern—
    Infinite passion, and the pain
Of finite hearts that yearn.

                              ROBERT BROWNING

"Fall, leaves, fall"

Fall, leaves, fall; die, flowers, away;
Lengthen night and shorten day;
Every leaf speaks bliss to me
Fluttering from the autumn tree.

I shall smile when wreaths of snow
Blossom where the rose should grow;
I shall sing when night's decay
Ushers in a drearier day.

EMILY BRONTË

"*Love is like the wild rose-briar*"

Love is like the wild rose-briar,
Friendship like the holly-tree—
The holly is dark when the rose-briar blooms
But which will bloom most constantly?

The wild rose-briar is sweet in spring,
Its summer blossoms scent the air;
Yet wait till winter comes again
And who will call the wild-briar fair?

Then scorn the silly rose-wreath now
And deck thee with the holly's sheen,
That when December blights thy brow
He still may leave thy garland green.

EMILY BRONTË

"*Shall Earth no more inspire thee?*"

Shall Earth no more inspire thee,
Thou lonely dreamer now?
Since passion may not fire thee
Shall Nature cease to bow?

Thy mind is ever moving
In regions dark to thee;
Recall its useless roving—
Come back and dwell with me.

I know my mountain-breezes
Enchant and soothe thee still—

I know my sunshine pleases
Despite thy wayward will.

When day with evening blending
Sinks from the summer sky,
I've seen thy spirit bending
In fond idolatry.

I've watched thee every hour—
I know my mighty sway—
I know my magic power
To drive thy griefs away.

Few hearts to mortals given
On earth so wildly pine
Yet none would ask a Heaven
More like the Earth than thine.

Then let my winds caress thee—
Thy comrade let me be—
Since nought beside can bless thee
Return and dwell with me.

EMILY BRONTË

"Silent is the House"

Silent is the House—all are laid asleep;
One, alone, looks out o'er the snow-wreaths deep;
Watching every cloud, dreading every breeze
That whirls the 'wildering drifts and bends the groaning trees.

Cheerful is the hearth, soft the matted floor;
Not one shivering gust creeps through pane or door;
The little lamp burns straight, its rays shoot strong and far:
I trim it well to be the Wanderer's guiding-star.

Frown my haughty sire; chide my angry dame,
Set your slaves to spy, threaten me with shame:
But neither sire nor dame, nor prying serf shall know
What angel nightly tracks that waste of winter snow.

What I love shall come like visitant of air,
Safe in secret power from lurking human snare;
Who loves me, no word of mine shall e'er betray,
Though for faith unstained my life must forfeit pay.

Burn, then, little lamp; glimmer straight and clear—
Hush! a rustling wing stirs, methinks, the air:
He for whom I wait, thus ever comes to me;
Strange Power! I trust thy might; trust thou my constancy.

EMILY BRONTË

Requiescat

Strew on her roses, roses,
   And never a spray of yew!
In quiet she reposes;
   Ah, would that I did too!

Her mirth the world required;
   She bathed it in smiles of glee.
But her heart was tired, tired,
   And now they let her be.

Her life was turning, turning,
   In mazes of heat and sound.
But for peace her soul was yearning,
   And now peace laps her round.

Her cabin'd, ample spirit,
   It flutter'd and fail'd for breath.
Tonight it doth inherit
   The vasty hall of death.

MATTHEW ARNOLD

Meeting

Again I see my bliss at hand,
The town, the lake are here;
My Marguerite smiles upon the strand,
Unalter'd with the year.

I know that graceful figure fair,
That cheek of languid hue;
I know that soft, enkerchief'd hair,
And those sweet eyes of blue.

Again I spring to make my choice;
Again in tones of ire
I hear a God's tremendous voice:
"Be counsell'd, and retire."

Ye guiding Powers who join and part,
What would ye have with me?
Ah, warn some more ambitious heart,
And let the peaceful be!

MATTHEW ARNOLD

To Marguerite

Yes! in the sea of life enisled,
With echoing straits between us thrown,
Dotting the shoreless watery wild,
We mortal millions live *alone*.
The islands feel the enclasping flow,
And then their endless bounds they know.

But when the moon their hollows lights,
And they are swept by balms of spring,
And in their glens, on starry nights,
The nightingales divinely sing;
And lovely notes, from shore to shore,
Across the sounds and channels pour—

Oh! then a longing like despair
Is to their farthest caverns sent;
For surely once, they feel, we were
Parts of a single continent!
Now round us spreads the watery plain—
Oh might our marges meet again!

Who order'd, that their longing's fire
Should be, as soon as kindled, cool'd?
Who renders vain their deep desire?—
A God, a God their severance ruled!
And bade betwixt their shores to be
The unplumb'd, salt, estranging sea.

MATTHEW ARNOLD

The Orphan's Song

I had a little bird,
I took it from the nest;
I prest it, and blest it,
And nursed it in my breast.

I set it on the ground,
I danced round and round,
And sang about it so cheerly,
With "Hey my little bird, and ho my little bird,
And oh but I love thee dearly!"

I make a little feast
Of food soft and sweet,
I hold it in my breast,
And coax it to eat;

I pit, and I pat,
I call it this and that,
And sing about it so cheerly,
With "Hey my little bird, and ho my little bird,
And ho but I love thee dearly!"

I may kiss, I may sing,
But I can't make it feed,
It taketh no heed
Of any pleasant thing.

I scolded, and I socked,
But it minded not a whit,
Its little mouth was locked,
And I could not open it.

Tho' with pit, and with pat,
And with this, and with that,
I sang about it so cheerly,
And "Hey my little bird, and ho my little bird,
And ho but I love thee dearly."

But when the day was done,
And the room was at rest,
And I sat all alone
With my birdie in my breast,

And the light had fled,
And not a sound was heard,
Then my little bird
Lifted up its head,

And the little mouth
Loosed its sullen pride,
And it opened, it opened,
With a yearning strong and wide.

Swifter than I speak
I brought it food once more,
But the poor little beak
Was locked as before.

I sat down again,
And not a creature stirred,
I laid the little bird
Again where it had lain;

And again when nothing stirred,
And not a word I said,
Then my little bird
Lifted up its head,
And the little beak
Loosed its stubborn pride,
And it opened, it opened,
With a yearning strong and wide.

It lay in my breast,
It uttered no cry,

'Twas famished, 'twas famished,
And I couldn't tell why.

I couldn't tell why,
But I saw that it would die,
For all that I kept dancing round and round,
And singing above it so cheerly,
With "Hey my little bird, and ho my little bird,
And ho but I love thee dearly!"

I never look sad,
I hear what people say,
I laugh when they are gay
And they think I am glad.

My tears never start,
I never say a word,
But I think that my heart
Is like that little bird.

Every day I read,
And I sing, and I play,
But thro' the long day
It taketh no heed.

It taketh no heed
Of any pleasant thing,
I know it doth not read,
I know it doth not sing.

With my mouth I read,
With my hands I play,
My shut heart is shut,
Coax it how you may.

You may coax it how you may
While the day is broad and bright,
But in the dead night
When the guests are gone away,

And no more the music sweet
Up the house doth pass,

Nor the dancing feet
Shake the nursery glass;

And I've heard my aunt
Along the corridor,
And my uncle gaunt
Lock his chamber door;

And upon the stair
All is hushed and still,
And the last wheel
Is silent in the square;

And the nurses snore,
And the dim sheets rise and fall,
And the lamplight's on the wall,
And the mouse is on the floor;

And the curtains of my bed
Are like a heavy cloud,
And the clock ticks loud,
And sounds are in my head;

And little Lizzie sleeps
Softly at my side,
It opens, it opens,
With a yearning strong and wide!

It yearns in my breast,
It utters no cry,
'Tis famished, 'tis famished,
And I feel that I shall die.

I feel that I shall die,
And none will know why,
Tho' the pleasant life is dancing round and round
And singing about me so cheerly,
With "Hey my little bird, and ho my little bird,
And ho but I love thee dearly!"

SYDNEY DOBELL

Sudden Light

I have been here before,
But when or how I cannot tell:
I know the grass beyond the door,
The sweet keen smell,
The sighing sound, the lights around the shore.

You have been mine before,—
How long ago I may not know:
But just when at that swallow's soar
Your neck turned so,
Some veil did fall,—I knew it all of yore.

Has this been thus before?
And shall not thus time's eddying flight
Still with our lives our love restore
In death's despite,
And day and night yield one delight once more?

DANTE GABRIEL ROSSETTI

The Woodspurge

The wind flapped loose, the wind was still,
Shaken out dead from tree and hill:
I had walked on at the wind's will,—
I sat now, for the wind was still.

Between my knees my forehead was,—
My lips, drawn in, said not Alas!
My hair was over in the grass,
My naked ears heard the day pass

My eyes, wide open, had the run
Of some ten weeds to fix upon;
Among those few, out of the sun,
The woodspurge flowered, three cups in one.

From perfect grief there need not be
Wisdom or even memory:
One thing then learnt remains to me,—
The woodspurge has a cup of three.

DANTE GABRIEL ROSSETTI

Silent Noon

Your hands lie open in the long fresh grass,—
    The finger-points look through like rosy blooms:
    Your eyes smile peace. The pasture gleams and glooms
'Neath billowing skies that scatter and amass.
All round our nest, far as the eye can pass,
    Are golden kingcup-fields with silver edge
    Where the cow-parsley skirts the hawthorn-hedge.
'Tis visible silence, still as the hour-glass.

Deep in the sun-searched growths the dragon-fly
Hangs like a blue thread loosened from the sky:—
    So this wing'd hour is dropt to us from above.
Oh! clasp we to our hearts, for deathless dower,
This close-companioned inarticulate hour
    When twofold silence was the song of love.

DANTE GABRIEL ROSSETTI

"Should thy love die"

    Should thy love die;
O bury it not under ice-blue eyes!
    And lips that deny,
With a scornful surprise,
The life it once lived in thy breast when it wore no disguise.

    Should thy love die;
O bury it where the sweet wild-flowers blow!
    And breezes go by,
With no whisper of woe;

And strange feet cannot guess of the anguish that slumbers
    below.

    Should thy love die;
  O wander once more to the haunt of the bee!
    Where the foliaged sky
  Is most sacred to see,
And thy being first felt its wild birth like a wind-wakened
    tree.

    Should thy love die;
  O dissemble it! smile! let the rose hide the thorn!
    While the lark sings on high,
  And no thing looks forlorn,
Bury it, bury it, bury it where it was born.

GEORGE MEREDITH

"We saw the swallows"

We saw the swallows gathering in the sky,
And in the osier-isle we heard their noise.
We had not to look back on summer joys,
Or forward to a summer of bright dye:
But in the largeness of the evening earth
Our spirits grew as we went side by side.
The hour became her husband and my bride.
Love, that had robbed us so, thus blessed our dearth!
The pilgrims of the year waxed very loud
In multitudinous chatterings, as the flood
Full brown came from the West, and like pale blood
Expanded to the upper crimson cloud.
Love, that had robbed us of immortal things,
This little moment mercifully gave,
Where I have seen across the twilight wave
The swan sail with her young beneath her wings.

GEORGE MEREDITH

osier = willow

Summer

Winter is cold-hearted,
Spring is yea and nay,
Autumn is a weathercock
Blown every way.
Summer days for me
When every leaf is on its tree;

When Robin's not a beggar,
And Jenny Wren's a bride,
And larks hang singing, singing, singing,
Over the wheat-fields wide,
And anchored lilies ride,
And the pendulum spider
Swings from side to side;

And blue-black beetles transact business,
And gnats fly in a host,
And furry caterpillars hasten
That no time be lost,
And moths grow fat and thrive,
And ladybirds arrive.

Before green apples blush,
Before green nuts embrown,
Why one day in the country
Is worth a month in town;
Is worth a day and a year
Of the dusty, musty, lag-last fashion
That days drone elsewhere.

CHRISTINA ROSSETTI

The Bourne

Underneath the growing grass,
Underneath the living flowers,
Deeper than the sound of showers:
There we shall not count the hours
By the shadows as they pass.

Youth and health will be but vain,
　Beauty reckoned of no worth:
　There a very little girth
　Can hold round what once the earth
Seemed too narrow to contain.

CHRISTINA ROSSETTI

Echo

Come to me in the silence of the night;
　Come in the speaking silence of a dream;
Come with soft rounded cheeks and eyes as bright
　As sunlight on a stream;
　　Come back in tears,
O memory, hope, love of finished years.

O dream how sweet, too sweet, too bitter sweet,
　Whose wakening should have been in Paradise,
Where souls brimfull of love abide and meet;
　Where thirsting longing eyes
　　Watch the slow door
That opening, letting in, lets out no more.

Yet come to me in dreams, that I may live
　My very life again though cold in death:
Come back to me in dreams, that I may give
　Pulse for pulse, breath for breath:
　　Speak low, lean low,
As long ago, my love, how long ago.

CHRISTINA ROSSETTI

The Wizard's Funeral

For me, for me, two horses wait,
Two horses stand before my gate:
The vast black plumes on high are cast,
Their black manes swing in the midnight blast,
Red sparkles from their eyes fly fast.

But can they drag the hearse behind,
Whose black plumes mystify the wind?
What a thing for this heap of bones and hair!
Despair, despair!
Yet think of half the world's winged shapes
Which have come to thee wondering:
At thee the terrible idiot gapes,
At thee the running devil japes,
And angels stoop to thee and sing
From the soft midnight that enwraps
Their limbs, so gently, sadly fair;—
Thou seest the stars shine through their hair.
The blast again, ho, ho, the blast!
I go to a mansion that shall outlast;
And the stoled priest who steps before
Shall turn and welcome me at the door.

                              R. W. DIXON

Anticipation

I set my heart to sing of leaves,
    Ere buds had felt the March wind blow:
I laid my head and dreamt of sheaves,
    Ere seedsmen had the heart to sow:
I fancied swallows at the eaves,
    And found old nests in pendent snow.

I dreamt a scent of daffodils,
    When frosty shone the village tiles:
Of flowery perfume from the hills,
    When ice had bound the mere for miles:
Of kingcups yellowing all the rills,
    When snowdrift silted up the stiles.

I found a barren bush of thorn,
    Where hung last year the sweet field-rose:
I said, no hint of purple morn
    The chambers of the east disclose:
Poor heart, poor song, poor pinions torn,
    Flutter and perish in the snows.

I said, a winter, huge and deep,
　　Crawls on the bitter, hungry plain:
Why should I dream, who cannot sleep,
　　Or hope to understand the pain,
Which rolls the doleful tears I weep,
　　That Spring is dead, that Love is slain?

WARREN DE TABLEY

The Sundew

A little marsh-plant, yellow green,
And pricked at lip with tender red.
Tread close, and either way you tread
Some faint black water jets between
Lest you should bruise the curious head.

A live thing maybe; who shall know?
The summer knows and suffers it;
For the cool moss is thick and sweet
Each side, and saves the blossom so
That it lives out the long June heat.

The deep scent of the heather burns
About it; breathless though it be,
Bow down and worship; more than we
Is the least flower whose life returns,
Least weed renascent in the sea.

We are vexed and cumbered in earth's sight
With wants, with many memories;
These see their mother what she is,
Glad-growing, till August leave more bright
The apple-coloured cranberries.

Wind blows and bleaches the strong grass,
Blown all one way to shelter it
From trample of strayed kine, with feet
Felt heavier than the moorhen was,
Strayed up past patches of wild wheat.

You call it sundew: how it grows,
If with its colour it have breath,
If life taste sweet to it, if death
Pain its soft petal, no man knows:
Man has no sight or sense that saith.

My sundew, grown of gentle days,
In these green miles the spring begun
Thy growth ere April had half done
With the soft secret of her ways
Or June made ready for the sun.

O red-lipped mouth of marsh-flower,
I have a secret halved with thee.
The name that is love's name to me
Thou knowest, and the face of her
Who is my festival to see.

The hard sun, as thy petals knew,
Coloured the heavy moss-water:
Thou wert not worth green midsummer
Nor fit to live to August blue,
O sundew, not remembering her.

ALGERNON CHARLES SWINBURNE

The Going

Why did you give no hint that night
That quickly after the morrow's dawn,
And calmly, as if indifferent quite,
You would close your term here, up and be gone
        Where I could not follow
        With wing of swallow
To gain one glimpse of you ever anon!

        Never to bid good-bye,
        Or lip me the softest call,
Or utter a wish for a word, while I
Saw morning harden upon the wall,
        Unmoved, unknowing

That your great going
Had place that moment, and altered all.

Why do you make me leave the house
And think for a breath it is you I see
At the end of the alley of bending boughs
Where so often at dusk you used to be;
 Till in darkening dankness
 The yawning blankness
Of the perspective sickens me!

 You were she who abode
 By those red-veined rocks far West,
You were the swan-necked one who rode
Along the beetling Beeny Crest,
 And, reining nigh me,
 Would muse and eye me,
While life unrolled us its very best.

Why, then, latterly did we not speak,
Did we not think of those days long dead,
And ere your vanishing strive to seek
That time's renewal? We might have said,
 "In this bright spring weather
 We'll visit together
Those places that once we visited."

 Well, well! All's past amend,
 Unchangeable. It must go.
I seem but a dead man held on end
To sink down soon. . . . O you could not know
 That such swift fleeing
 No soul foreseeing—
Not even I—would undo me so!

THOMAS HARDY

After a Journey

Hereto I come to view a voiceless ghost;
 Whither, O whither will its whim now draw me?
Up the cliff, down, till I'm lonely, lost,

And the unseen waters' ejaculations awe me.
Where you will next be there's no knowing,
     Facing round about me everywhere,
          With your nut-coloured hair,
And gray eyes, and rose-flush coming and going.

Yes: I have re-entered your olden haunts at last;
     Through the years, through the dead scenes I have tracked you;
What have you now found to say of our past—
     Scanned across the dark space wherein I have lacked you?
Summer gave us sweets, but autumn wrought division?
     Things were not lastly as firstly well
          With us twain, you tell?
But all's closed now, despite Time's derision.

I see what you are doing: you are leading me on
     To the spots we knew when we haunted here together,
The waterfall, above which the mist-bow shone
     At the then fair hour in the then fair weather,
And the cave just under, with a voice still so hollow
     That it seems to call out to me from forty years ago,
          When you were all aglow,
And not the thin ghost that I now frailly follow!

Ignorant of what there is flitting here to see,
     The waked birds preen and the seals flop lazily;
Soon you will have, Dear, to vanish from me,
     For the stars close their shutters and the dawn whitens hazily.
Trust me, I mind not, though Life lours,
     The bringing me here; nay, bring me here again!
          I am just the same as when
Our days were a joy, and our paths through flowers.

                                        THOMAS HARDY

Lines

TO A MOVEMENT IN MOZART'S E-FLAT SYMPHONY

     Show me again the time
     When in the Junetide's prime
We flew by meads and mountains northerly!—

Yea, to such freshness, fairness, fulness, fineness, freeness,
  Love lures life on.

  Show me again the day
  When from the sandy bay
We looked together upon the pestered sea!—
Yea, to such surging, swaying, sighing, swelling, shrinking,
  Love lures life on.

  Show me again the hour
  When by the pinnacled tower
We eyed each other and feared futurity!—
Yea, to such bodings, broodings, beatings, blanchings, blessings,
  Love lures life on.

  Show me again just this:
  The moment of that kiss
Away from the prancing folk, by the strawberry-tree!—
Yea, to such rashness, ratheness, rareness, ripeness, richness,
  Love lures life on.

THOMAS HARDY

During Wind and Rain

  They sing their dearest songs—
  He, she, all of them—yea,
  Treble and tenor and bass,
    And one to play;
  With the candles mooning each face. . . .
    Ah, no; the years O!
How the sick leaves reel down in throngs!

  They clear the creeping moss—
  Elders and juniors—aye,
  Making the pathways neat
    And the garden gay;
  And they build a shady seat. . . .
    Ah, no; the years, the years;
See, the white storm-birds wing across!

They are blithely breakfasting all—
Men and maidens—yea,
Under the summer tree,
   With a glimpse of the bay,
While pet fowl come to the knee. . . .
      Ah, no; the years O!
And the rotten rose is ript from the wall.

They change to a high new house,
He, she, all of them—aye,
Clocks and carpets and chairs
   On the lawn all day,
And the brightest things that are theirs. . . .
      Ah, no; the years, the years;
Down their carved names the rain-drop ploughs.

THOMAS HARDY

Spring and Fall

Margaret, are you grieving
Over Goldengrove unleaving?
Leaves, like the things of man, you
With your fresh thoughts care for, can you?
Ah! as the heart grows older
It will come to such sights colder
By and by, nor spare a sigh
Though worlds of wanwood leafmeal lie;
And yet you will weep and know why.
Now no matter, child, the name:
Sorrow's springs are the same.
Nor mouth had, no nor mind, expressed
What heart heard of, ghost guessed:
It is the blight man was born for,
It is Margaret you mourn for.

GERARD MANLEY HOPKINS

Binsey Poplars

My aspens dear, whose airy cages quelled,
Quelled or quenched in leaves the leaping sun,
All felled, felled, are all felled;
    Of a fresh and following folded rank
        Not spared, not one
        That dandled a sandalled
       Shadow that swam or sank
On meadow and river and wind-wandering weed-winding
    bank.

  O if we but knew what we do
      When we delve or hew—
    Hack and rack the growing green!
      Since country is so tender
    To touch, her being so slender,
    That, like this sleek and seeing ball
    But a prick will make no eye at all,
    Where we, even where we mean
      To mend her we end her,
    When we hew or delve:
After-comers cannot guess the beauty been.
  Ten or twelve, only ten or twelve
    Strokes of havoc unselve
      The sweet especial scene,
    Rural scene, a rural scene,
    Sweet especial rural scene.

                    GERARD MANLEY HOPKINS

Peace

When will you ever, Peace, wild wooddove, shy wings shut,
Your round me roaming end, and under be my boughs?
When, when, Peace, will you, Peace? I'll not play hypocrite
To own my heart: I yield you do come sometimes; but
That piecemeal peace is poor peace. What pure peace allows
Alarms of wars, the daunting wars, the death of it?

O surely, reaving Peace, my Lord should leave in lieu
Some good! And so he does Ieave Patience exquisite,
That plumes to Peace thereafter. And when Peace here does house
He comes with work to do, he does not come to coo,
      He comes to brood and sit.

GERARD MANLEY HOPKINS

"Tell me not here"

Tell me not here, it needs not saying,
  What tune the enchantress plays
In aftermaths of soft September
  Or under blanching mays,
For she and I were long acquainted
  And I knew all her ways.

On russet floors, by waters idle,
  The pine lets fall its cone;
The cuckoo shouts all day at nothing
  In leafy dells alone;
And traveller's joy beguiles in autumn
  Hearts that have lost their own.

On acres of the seeded grasses
  The changing burnish heaves;
Or marshalled under moons of harvest
  Stand still all night the sheaves;
Or beeches strip in storms for winter
  And stain the wind with leaves.

Possess, as I possessed a season,
  The countries I resign,
Where over elmy plains the highway
  Would mount the hills and shine,
And full of shade the pillared forest
  Would murmur and be mine.

For nature, heartless, witless nature,
  Will neither care nor know
What stranger's feet may find the meadow

And trespass there and go,
Nor ask amid the dews of morning
If they are mine or no.

A. E. HOUSMAN

"White in the moon"

White in the moon the long road lies,
    The moon stands blank above;
White in the moon the long road lies
    That leads me from my love.

Still hangs the hedge without a gust,
    Still, still the shadows stay:
My feet upon the moonlit dust
    Pursue the ceaseless way.

The world is round, so travellers tell,
    And straight though reach the track,
Trudge on, trudge on, 'twill all be well,
    The way will guide one back.

But ere the circle homeward hies
    Far, far must it remove:
White in the moon the long road lies
    That leads me from my love.

A. E. HOUSMAN

Solomon to Sheba

Sang Solomon to Sheba,
    And kissed her dusky face,
"All day long from mid-day
    We have talked in the one place,
All day long from shadowless noon
    We have gone round and round
In the narrow theme of love
    Like an old horse in a pound."

To Solomon sang Sheba,
Planted on his knees,
"If you had broached a matter
That might the learnèd please,
You had before the sun had thrown
Our shadows on the ground
Discovered that my thoughts, not it,
Are but a narrow pound."

Said Solomon to Sheba,
And kissed her Arab eyes,
"There's not a man or woman
Born under the skies
Dare match in learning with us two,
And all day long we have found
There's not a thing but love can make
The world a narrow pound."

WILLIAM BUTLER YEATS

A Last Confession

What lively lad most pleasured me
Of all that with me lay?
I answer that I gave my soul
And loved in misery,
But had great pleasure with a lad
That I loved bodily.

Flinging from his arms I laughed
To think his passion such
He fancied that I gave a soul
Did but our bodies touch,
And laughed upon his breast to think
Beast gave beast as much.

I gave what other women gave
That stepped out of their clothes,
But when this soul, its body off,
Naked to naked goes,

He it has found shall find therein
What none other knows,

And give his own and take his own
And rule in his own right;
And though it loved in misery
Close and cling so tight,
There's not a bird of day that dare
Extinguish that delight.

WILLIAM BUTLER YEATS

The Ghost

"Who knocks?" "I, who was beautiful,
 Beyond all dreams to restore,
I, from the roots of the dark thorn am hither.
 And knock on the door."

"Who speaks?" "I— once was my speech
 Sweet as the bird's on the air,
When echo lurks by the waters to heed;
 'Tis I speak thee fair."

"Dark is the hour!" "Ay, and cold."
 "Lone is my house." "Ah, but mine?"
"Sight, touch, lips, eyes yearned in vain."
 "Long dead these to thine. . . ."

Silence. Still faint on the porch
 Brake the flames of the stars.
In gloom groped a hope-wearied hand
 Over keys, bolts, and bars.

A face peered. All the grey night
 In chaos of vacancy shone;
Nought but vast sorrow was there—
 The sweet cheat gone.

WALTER DE LA MARE

"She said"

She said, "I will come back again
    As soon as breaks the morn."
But the lark was wearying of the blue,
    The dew dry on the thorn;
    And all was still forlorn.

She said, "I will come back again,
    At the first quick stroke of noon."
But the birds were hid in the shade from the heat
    When the clock tolled, *No: but soon!*
    And then beat slowly on.

She said, "Yes, I'll be back again
    Before the sun has set."
But the sweetest promises often made
    Are the easiest to forget,
    No matter grief and fret. . . .

That moon, now silvering the east,
    One shadow casts—my own.
Thought I, My friend, how often we
Have shared this solitude. And see,
    Midnight will soon draw on,
When the last leaf of hope is fallen,
And silence haunts heart's vacancy,
    And even pining's done.

WALTER DE LA MARE

To a Candle

Burn stilly, thou; and come with me.
I'll screen thy rays. Now . . . Look, and see,
    Where, like a flower furled,
    Sealed from this busy world,
Tranquil brow, and lid, and lip,
One I love lies here asleep.

Low upon her pillow is
A head of such strange loveliness—
Gilded-brown, unwoven hair—
That dread springs up to see it there:
Lest so profound a trance should be
Death's momentary alchemy.

Venture closer, then. Thy light
Be little day to this small night!
Fretting through her lids it makes
The lashes stir on those pure cheeks;
The scarcely-parted lips, it seems,
Pine, but in vain, to tell her dreams.

Every curve and hollow shows
In faintest shadow—mouth and nose;
Pulsing beneath the silken skin
The milk-blue blood rills out and in:
A bird's might be that slender bone,
Magic itself to ponder on.

Time hath spread its nets in vain;
The child she was is home again;
Veiled with Sleep's seraphic grace.
How innocent yet how wise a face!
Mutely entreating, it seems to sigh,—
"Love made me. It is only I.

"Love made this house wherein there dwells
A thing divine, and homeless else.
Not mine the need to ponder why
In this sweet prison I exult and sigh.
Not mine to bid you hence. God knows
It was for joy he shaped the rose."

See, she stirs. A hand at rest
Slips from above that gentle breast,
White as winter-mounded snows,
Summer-sweet as that wild rose . . .
Thou lovely thing! Ah, welladay!
Candle, I dream. Come, come away!

WALTER DE LA MARE

Gloire de Dijon

When she rises in the morning
I linger to watch her;
She spreads the bath-cloth underneath the window
And the sunbeams catch her
Glistening white on the shoulders,
While down her sides the mellow
Golden shadow glows as
She stoops to the sponge, and her swung breasts
Sway like full-blown yellow
Gloire de Dijon roses.

She drips herself with water, and her shoulders
Glisten as silver, they crumple up
Like wet and falling roses, and I listen
For the sluicing of their rain-dishevelled petals.
In the window full of sunlight
Concentrates her golden shadow
Fold on fold, until it glows as
Mellow as the glory roses.

D. H. LAWRENCE

A Young Wife

The pain of loving you
Is almost more than I can bear.

I walk in fear of you.
The darkness starts up where
You stand, and the night comes through
Your eyes when you look at me.

Ah never before did I see
The shadows that live in the sun!

Now every tall glad tree
Turns round its back to the sun
And looks down on the ground, to see
The shadow it used to shun.

At the foot of each glowing thing
A night lies looking up.

Oh, and I want to sing
And dance, but I can't lift up
My eyes from the shadows: dark
They lie spilt round the cup.

What is it?—Hark
The faint fine seethe in the air!

Like the seething sound in a shell!
It is death still seething where
The wild-flower shakes its bell
And the skylark twinkles blue—

The pain of loving you
Is almost more than I can bear.

                          D. H. LAWRENCE

Counting the Beats

You, love, and I,
(He whispers) you and I,
And if no more than only you and I
What care you or I?

Counting the beats,
Counting the slow heart beats,
The bleeding to death of time in slow heart beats,
Wakeful they lie.

Cloudless day,
Night, and a cloudless day;
Yet the huge storm will burst upon their heads one day
From a bitter sky.

Where shall we be,
(She whispers) where shall we be,

When death strikes home, O where then shall we be
Who were you and I?

Not there but here,
(He whispers) only here,
As we are, here, together, now and here,
Always you and I.

Counting the beats,
Counting the slow heart beats,
The bleeding to death of time in slow heart beats,
Wakeful they lie.

ROBERT GRAVES

DEVOTIONAL LYRICS

"I sing of a maiden"

I sing of a maiden
    That is makeless;
King of all kings
    To her son she ches.

He came all so still
    Where his mother was,
As dew in April
    That falleth on the grass.

He came all so still
    To his mother's bower,
As dew in April
    That falleth on the flower.

He came all so still
    Where his mother lay,
As dew in April
    That falleth on the spray.

Mother and maiden
    Was never none but she;
Well may such a lady
    Godès mother be.

ANON.

makeless = matchless
ches = chose

"Lullay my liking"

Lullay my liking, my dear
    son, my sweeting;
Lullay my dear heart, mine
    own dear darling!

I saw a fair maiden
    Sitten and sing:

215

She lullèd a little child,
  A sweetè lording:

  Lullay my liking, my dear
    son, my sweeting;
  Lullay my dear heart, mine
    own dear darling!

That eternal lord is he
  That made allè thing;
Of allè lordès he is Lord,
  Of allè kingès king.

There was mickle melody
  At that childès birth:
Although they were in heaven's bliss
  They madè mickle mirth.

Angels bright they sang that night
  And saiden to that child
"Blessed be thou, and so be she
  That is both meek and mild."

Pray we now to that child,
  And to his mother dear,
God grant them all his blessing
  That now maken cheer.

ANON.

Coventry Carol

Lully, lulla, thou little tiny child,
By by, lully lullay.
O sisters too,
How may we do
  For to preserve this day
This poor youngling,
For whom we do sing,
  By by, lully lullay?

Herod, the king,
In his raging,
    Chargèd he hath this day
His men of might,
In his own sight,
    All young childrén to slay.

That woe is me,
Poor child for thee!
    And ever morn and day,
For thy parting
Neither say nor sing
    By by, lully lullay!

                              ANON.

The Cherry-Tree Carol

Joseph was an old man,
    and an old man was he,
When he wedded Mary,
    in the land of Galilee.

Joseph and Mary walked
    through an orchard good,
Where was cherries and berries,
    so red as any blood.

Joseph and Mary walked
    through an orchard green,
Where was berries and cherries,
    as thick as might be seen.

O then bespoke Mary,
    so meek and so mild:
"Pluck me one cherry, Joseph,
    for I am with child."

O then bespoke Joseph,
    with words most unkind:
"Let him pluck thee a cherry
    that brought thee with child."

O then bespoke the babe,
   within his mother's womb:
"Bow down then the tallest tree,
   for my mother to have some."

Then bowed down the highest tree
   unto his mother's hand;
Then she cried, "See, Joseph,
   I have cherries at command."

O then bespake Joseph:
   "I have done Mary wrong;
But cheer up, my dearest,
   and be not cast down."

Then Mary plucked a cherry,
   as red as the blood,
Then Mary went home
   with her heavy load.

Then Mary took her babe,
   and sat him on her knee,
Saying, "My dear son, tell me
   what this world will be."

"O I shall be as dead, mother,
   as the stones in the wall;
O the stones in the streets, mother,
   shall mourn for me all.

"Upon Easter-day, mother,
   my uprising shall be;
O the sun and the moon, mother,
   shall both rise with me."

                 ANON.

"The Holly and the Ivy"

The holly and the ivy,
When they are both full grown,
Of all the trees that are in the wood,
The holly bears the crown:

The rising of the sun
And the running of the deer,
The playing of the merry organ,
Sweet singing in the choir.

The holly bears a blossom,
As white as the lily flower,
And Mary bore sweet Jesus Christ,
To be our sweet Saviour.

The holly bears a berry,
As red as any blood,
And Mary bore sweet Jesus Christ
To do poor sinners good.

The holly bears a prickle,
As sharp as any thorn,
And Mary bore sweet Jesus Christ
On Christmas day in the morn.

The holly bears a bark,
As bitter as any gall,
And Mary bore sweet Jesus Christ
For to redeem us all.

The holly and the ivy,
When they are both full grown,
Of all the trees that are in the wood,
The holly bears the crown.

ANON.

"Christ, my Beloved"

Christ, my Beloved which still doth feed
   Among the flowers, having delight
     Among his faithful lilies,
Doth take great care for me indeed,
   And I again with all my might
     Will do what so his will is.

My love in me and I in him,
  Conjoined by love, will still abide
    Among the faithful lilies
Till day do break, and truth do dim
  All shadows dark and cause them slide,
    According as his will is.

WILLIAM BALDWIN

New Prince, New Pomp

Behold a silly, tender babe,
  In freezing winter night,
In homely manger trembling lies;
  Alas! a piteous sight.

The inns are full; no man will yield
  This little pilgrim bed;
But forced he is with silly beasts
  In crib to shroud his head.

Despise him not for lying there;
  First what he is inquire:
An orient pearl is often found
  In depth of dirty mire.

Weigh not his crib, his wooden dish,
  Nor beasts that by him feed;
Weigh not his mother's poor attire,
  Nor Joseph's simple weed.

The stable is a prince's court,
  The crib his chair of state;
The beasts are parcel of his pomp,
  The wooden dish his plate.

The persons in that poor attire
  His royal liveries wear;
The Prince himself is come from heaven:
  This pomp is prizèd there.

silly = simple

With joy approach, O Christian wight;
    Do homage to thy King;
And highly praise his humble pomp,
    Which he from heaven doth bring.

ROBERT SOUTHWELL

"Awake, awake!"

Awake, awake! thou heavy sprite
    That sleep'st the deadly sleep of sin!
Rise now and walk the ways of light,
    'Tis not too late yet to begin.
Seek heaven early, seek it late;
True Faith finds still an open gate.

Get up, get up, thou leaden man!
    Thy track, to endless joy or pain,
Yields but the model of a span:
    Yet burns out thy life's lamp in vain!
One minute bounds thy bane or bliss;
Then watch and labour while time is.

THOMAS CAMPION

"Adieu, farewell earth's bliss"

Adieu, farewell earth's bliss,
This world uncertain is,
Fond are life's lustful joys,
Death proves them all but toys,
None from his darts can fly,
I am sick, I must die:
    Lord have mercy on us.

Rich men, trust not in wealth,
Gold cannot buy you health,
Physic himself must fade.
All things, to end are made,
The plague full swift goes by,

I am sick, I must die:
    Lord have mercy on us.

Beauty is but a flower,
Which wrinkles will devour,
Brightness falls from the air,
Queens have died young, and fair,
Dust hath closed Helen's eye.
I am sick, I must die:
    Lord have mercy on us.

Strength stoops unto the grave,
Worms feed on Hector brave,
Swords may not fight with fate,
Earth still holds ope her gate.
Come, come, the bells do cry.
I am sick, I must die:
    Lord have mercy on us.

Wit with his wantonness,
Tasteth death's bitterness:
Hell's executioner,
Hath no ears for to hear
What vain art can reply.
I am sick, I must die:
    Lord have mercy on us.

Haste therefore each degree,
To welcome destiny:
Heaven is our heritage,
Earth but a players' stage,
Mount we unto the sky.
I am sick, I must die:
    Lord have mercy on us.

                THOMAS NASHE

A Contemplation upon Flowers

Brave flowers—that I could gallant it like you,
    And be as little vain!
You come abroad, and make a harmless show,

And to your beds of earth again.
You are not proud: you know your birth:
For your embroidered garments are from earth.

You do obey your months and times, but I
        Would have it ever spring:
My fate would know no winter, never die,
        Nor think of such a thing.
Oh, that I could my bed of earth but view
And smile, and look as cheerfully as you!

Oh, teach me to see death and not to fear,
        But rather to take truce!
How often have I seen you at a bier,
        And there look fresh and spruce!
You fragrant flowers, then teach me, that my breath
Like yours may sweeten and perfume my death.

                                    HENRY KING

His Litany to the Holy Spirit

        In the hour of my distress,
        When temptations me oppress,
        And when I my sins confess,
                Sweet Spirit comfort me!

        When I lie within my bed,
        Sick in heart and sick in head,
        And with doubts discomforted,
                Sweet Spirit comfort me!

        When the house doth sigh and weep,
        And the world is drown'd in sleep,
        Yet mine eyes the watch do keep;
                Sweet Spirit comfort me!

        When the artless doctor sees
        No one hope, but of his fees,
        And his skill runs on the lees;
                Sweet Spirit comfort me!

When his potion and his pill
Has, or none, or little skill,
Meet for nothing, but to kill;
          Sweet Spirit comfort me!

When the passing-bell doth toll,
And the Furies in a shoal
Come to fright a parting soul;
          Sweet Spirit comfort me!

When the tapers now burn blue,
And the comforters are few,
And that number more than true;
          Sweet Spirit comfort me!

When the priest his last hath prayed,
And I nod to what is said,
'Cause my speech is now decayed;
          Sweet Spirit comfort me!

When (God knows) I'm tossed about,
Either with despair, or doubt;
Yet before the glass be out,
          Sweet Spirit comfort me!

When the Tempter me pursu'th
With the sins of all my youth,
And half damns me with untruth;
          Sweet Spirit comfort me!

When the flames and hellish cries
Fright mine ears, and fright mine eyes,
And all terrors me surprise;
          Sweet Spirit comfort me!

When the Judgment is reveal'd,
And that open'd which was seal'd,
When to Thee I have appeal'd;
          Sweet Spirit comfort me!

                    ROBERT HERRICK

Prayer

Prayer, the Church's banquet, Angel's age,
  God's breath in man returning to his birth,
  The soul in paraphrase, heart in pilgrimage,
The Christian plummet sounding heaven and earth;

Engine against th' Almighty, sinner's tower,
  Reversèd thunder, Christ-side-piercing spear,
  The six days' world-transposing in an hour,
A kind of tune, which all things hear and fear;

Softness, and peace, and joy, and love, and bliss,
  Exalted Manna, gladness of the best,
  Heaven in ordinary, men well drest,
The Milky Way, the bird of Paradise,

  Church-bells beyond the stars heard, the soul's blood,
  The land of spices, something understood.

GEORGE HERBERT

Peace

Sweet Peace, where dost thou dwell? I humbly crave,
          Let me once know.
      I sought thee in a secret cave,
          And ask'd, if Peace were there.
A hollow wind did seem to answer, No:
          Go seek elsewhere.

I did; and going did a rainbow note:
          Surely, thought I,
      This is the lace of Peace's coat:
          I will search out the matter.
But while I look'd, the clouds immediately
          Did break and scatter.

Then went I to a garden, and did spy
          A gallant flower,

The Crown Imperial: Sure, said I,
      Peace at the root must dwell.
But when I digg'd, I saw a worm devour
      What show'd so well.

At length I met a reverend good old man:
      Whom when for Peace
I did demand, he thus began:
      There was a Prince of old
At Salem dwelt, who lived with good increase
      Of flock and fold.

He sweetly lived; yet sweetness did not save
      His life from foes.
But after death out of his grave
      There sprang twelve stalks of wheat:
Which many wondering at, got some of those
      To plant and set.

It prosper'd strangely, and did soon disperse
      Through all the earth:
For they that taste it do rehearse
      That virtue lies therein;
A secret virtue, bringing peace and mirth
      By flight of sin.

Take of this grain, which in my garden grows,
      And grows for you;
Make bread of it: and that repose
      And peace, which every where
With so much earnestness you do pursue,
      Is only there.

GEORGE HERBERT

The Flower

How fresh, O Lord, how sweet and clean
Are thy returns! even as the flowers in spring;
    To which, besides their own demean,
The late-past frosts tributes of pleasure bring.

Grief melts away
Like snow in May,
As if there were no such cold thing.

Who would have thought my shrivell'd heart
Could have recover'd greenness? It was gone
Quite under ground; as flowers depart
To see their Mother-root, when they have blown;
Where they together
All the hard weather,
Dead to the world, keep house unknown.

These are thy wonders, Lord of power,
Killing and quickening, bringing down to hell
And up to heaven in an hour;
Making a chiming of a passing bell.
We say amiss,
This or that is:
Thy Word is all, if we could spell.

O that I once past changing were,
Fast in thy Paradise, where no flower can wither!
Many a spring I shoot up fair,
Offering at heaven, growing and groaning thither:
Nor doth my flower
Want a spring-shower,
My sins and I joining together.

But while I grow in a straight line,
Still upwards bent, as if heaven were mine own,
Thy anger comes, and I decline:
What frost to that? what pole is not the zone
Where all things burn,
When thou dost turn,
And the least frown of thine is shown?

And now in age I bud again,
After so many deaths I live and write;
I once more smell the dew and rain,
And relish versing: O my only light,
It cannot be
That I am he,
On whom thy tempests fell at night.

These are thy wonders, Lord of love,
To make us see we are flowers that glide:
Which when we once can find and prove,
Thou hast a garden for us, where to bide.
Who would be more,
Swelling through store,
Forfeit their Paradise by their pride.

GEORGE HERBERT

Virtue

Sweet Day, so cool, so calm, so bright,
The bridal of the earth and sky,
The dew shall weep thy fall tonight;
For thou must die.

Sweet Rose, whose hue angry and brave
Bids the rash gazer wipe his eye,
Thy root is ever in its grave,
And thou must die.

Sweet Spring, full of sweet days and roses,
A box where sweets compacted lie,
My Music shows ye have your closes,
And all must die.

Only a sweet and virtuous soul,
Like season'd timber, never gives;
But though the whole world turn to coal,
Then chiefly lives.

GEORGE HERBERT

Peace

My soul, there is a country
Far beyond the stars,
Where stands a wingèd sentry
All skilful in the wars:

There, above noise and danger,
    Sweet Peace sits crown'd with smiles,
And One born in a manger
    Commands the beauteous files.
He is thy gracious Friend,
    And—O my soul awake!—
Did in pure love descend,
    To die here for thy sake.
If thou canst get but thither,
    There grows the flower of Peace,
The Rose that cannot wither,
    Thy fortress, and thy ease.
Leave then thy foolish ranges;
    For none can thee secure,
But One, who never changes,
    Thy God, thy life, thy cure.

HENRY VAUGHAN

Quickness

False life! a foil and no more, when
            Wilt thou be gone?
Thou foul deception of all men,
That would not have the true come on!

Thou art a moon-like toil; a blind
            Self-posing state;
A dark contest of waves and wind;
A mere tempestuous debate.

Life is a fix'd, discerning light,
            A knowing joy;
No chance, or fit; but ever bright,
And calm, and full, yet doth not cloy.

'Tis such a blissful thing, that still
            Doth vivify,
And shine and smile, and hath the skill
To please without eternity.

Thou art a toilsome mole, or less,
A moving mist.
But life is, what none can express,
A quickness, which my God hath kiss'd.

HENRY VAUGHAN

"Unfold! unfold!"

Unfold! unfold! Take in his light,
Who makes thy cares more short than night.
The joys which with his day-star rise
He deals to all but drowsy eyes;
And, what the men of this world miss,
Some drops and dews of future bliss.

Hark! how His winds have changed their note,
And with warm whispers call thee out!
The frosts are past, the storms are gone,
And backward life at last comes on.
The lofty groves in express joys
Reply unto the turtle's voice;
And here in dust and dirt, oh, here
The lilies of His love appear!

HENRY VAUGHAN

"To walk *abroad"*

To *walk* abroad is, not with eyes,
But thoughts, the fields to see and prize;
Else may the silent feet,
Like logs of wood,
Move up and down, and see no good,
Nor joy nor glory meet.

Ev'n carts and wheels their place do change,
But cannot see, though very strange
The glory that is by:
Dead puppets may

Move in the bright and glorious day,
  Yet not behold the sky.

And are not men than they more blind,
Who having eyes yet never find
  The bliss in which they move?
    Like statues dead
They up and down are carrièd,
  Yet neither see nor love.

To *walk* is by a thought to go,
To move in spirit to and fro,
  To mind the good we see,
    To taste the sweet,
Observing all the things we meet
  How choice and rich they be:

To note the beauty of the day,
And golden fields of corn survey;
  Admire each pretty flower
    With its sweet smell;
To praise their Maker, and to tell
  The marks of his great power:

To fly abroad, like active bees,
Among the hedges and the trees,
  To cull the dew that lies
    On every blade,
From every blossom, till we lade
  Our minds, as they their thighs:

Observe those rich and glorious things,
The rivers, meadows, woods, and springs,
  The fructifying sun;
    To note from far
The rising of each twinkling star
  For us his race to run.

A little child these well perceives,
Who, tumbling in green grass and leaves,
  May rich as kings be thought:
    But there's a sight

Which perfect manhood may delight,
  To which we shall be brought.

While in those pleasant paths we talk
'Tis *that* towards which at last we walk;
  For we may by degrees
    Wisely proceed
Pleasures of love and praise to heed,
  From viewing herbs and trees.

THOMAS TRAHERNE

The Pilgrim Song

Who would true valour see,
Let him come hither;
One here will constant be,
Come wind, come weather.
There's no discouragement
Shall make him once relent
His first avow'd intent,
To be a pilgrim.

Who so beset him round
With dismal stories,
Do but themselves confound;
His strength the more is.
No lion can him fright,
He'll with a giant fight,
But he will have a right
To be a pilgrim.

Hobgoblin, nor foul fiend,
Can daunt his spirit:
He knows, he at the end
Shall life inherit.
Then fancies fly away,
He'll fear not what men say,
He'll labour night and day
To be a pilgrim.

JOHN BUNYAN

"The spacious firmament on high"

The spacious firmament on high,
With all the blue ethereal sky,
And spangled heavens, a shining frame,
Their great Original proclaim.
The unwearied sun from day to day
Does his Creator's power display,
And publishes to every land
The works of an almighty hand.

Soon as the evening shades prevail
The moon takes up the wondrous tale,
And nightly to the listening earth
Repeats the story of her birth;
Whilst all the stars that round her burn
And all the planets in their turn,
Confirm the tidings, as they roll,
And spread the truth from pole to pole.

What though in solemn silence all
Move round the dark terrestrial ball;
What though nor real voice nor sound
Amid their radiant orbs be found;
In reason's ear they all rejoice,
And utter forth a glorious voice;
For ever singing as they shine,
"The hand that made us is divine."

JOSEPH ADDISON

"There is a land"

There is a land of pure delight
    Where saints immortal reign;
Infinite day excludes the night,
    And pleasures banish pain.

There everlasting spring abides,
    And never-withering flowers:
Death like a narrow sea divides
    This heav'nly land from ours.

Sweet fields beyond the swelling flood
  Stand dress'd in living green:
So to the Jews old Canaan stood,
  While Jordan rolled between.

But timorous mortals start and shrink
  To cross this narrow sea,
And linger shivering on the brink,
  And fear to launch away.

O could we make our doubts remove,
  These gloomy doubts that rise,
And see the Canaan that we love,
  With unbeclouded eyes;

Could we but climb where Moses stood,
  And view the landscape o'er,
Not Jordan's stream, nor death's cold flood,
  Should fright us from the shore.

                                ISAAC WATTS

"All the scenes of nature quicken"

All the scenes of nature quicken,
  By the genial spirit fanned;
And the painted beauties thicken,
  Coloured by the Master's hand;

Earth her vigour repossessing,
  As the blasts are held in ward,
Blessing heaped and pressed on blessing,
  Yield the measure of the Lord.

Cowslips seize upon the fallow,
  And the cardamine in white,
Where the cornflowers join the mallow,
  Joy and health and thrift unite.

Hark! aloud the blackbird whistles,
  With surrounding fragrance blest,

And the goldfinch in the thistles
Makes provision for her nest.

Prayer and praise be mine employment
Without grudging or regret:
Lasting life and long enjoyment
Are not here, and are not yet.

CHRISTOPHER SMART

"Christ, whose glory fills the skies"

Christ, whose glory fills the skies,
    Christ, the true, the only Light,
Sun of Righteousness, arise,
    Triumph o'er the shades of night;
Dayspring from on high, be near;
Daystar, in my heart appear.

Dark and cheerless is the morn
    Unaccompanied by thee;
Joyless is the day's return,
    Till thy mercy's beams I see;
Till they inward light impart,
Glad my eyes, and warm my heart.

Visit then this soul of mine,
    Pierce the gloom of sin and grief;
Fill me, radiancy divine,
    Scatter all my unbelief;
More and more thyself display,
Shining to the perfect day.

CHARLES WESLEY

"God moves in a mysterious way"

God moves in a mysterious way
    His wonders to perform;
He plants his footsteps in the sea,
    And rides upon the storm.

Deep in unfathomable mines
  Of never-failing skill
He treasures up his bright designs,
  And works his sovereign will.

Ye fearful saints, fresh courage take,
  The clouds ye so much dread
Are big with mercy, and shall break
  In blessings on your head.

Judge not the Lord by feeble sense,
  But trust him for his grace;
Behind a frowning providence
  He hides a smiling face.

His purposes will ripen fast,
  Unfolding every hour;
The bud may have a bitter taste,
  But sweet will be the flower.

Blind unbelief is sure to err,
  And scan his work in vain;
God is his own interpreter,
  And he will make it plain.

WILLIAM COWPER

"By cool Siloam's shady rill"

By cool Siloam's shady rill
  How sweet the lily grows!
How sweet the breath beneath the hill
  Of Sharon's dewy rose!

Lo, such the child whose early feet
  The paths of peace have trod;
Whose secret heart, with influence sweet,
  Is upward drawn to God.

By cool Siloam's shady rill
   The lily must decay;
The rose that blooms beneath the hill
   Must shortly fade away.

And soon, too soon, the wintry hour
   Of man's maturer age
Will shake the soul with sorrow's power,
   And stormy passion's rage.

O Thou, Whose infant feet were found
   Within Thy Father's shrine!
Whose years, with changeless virtue crown'd,
   Were all alike Divine;

Dependent on Thy bounteous breath,
   We seek Thy grace alone,
In childhood, manhood, age, and death,
   To keep us still Thine own!

               REGINALD HEBER

from
In Memoriam

Be near me when my light is low,
   When the blood creeps, and the nerves prick
   And tingle; and the heart is sick,
And all the wheels of Being slow.

Be near me when the sensuous frame
   Is rack'd with pangs that conquer trust;
   And Time, a maniac scattering dust,
And Life, a Fury slinging fame.

Be near me when my faith is dry,
   And men the flies of latter spring,
   That lay their eggs, and sting and sing
And weave their petty cells and die.

Be near me when I fade away,
    To point the term of human strife,
    And on the low dark verge of life
The twilight of eternal day.

ALFRED, LORD TENNYSON

from
The Prisoner

He comes with western winds, with evening's wandering airs,
With that clear dusk of heaven that brings the thickest stars;
Winds take a pensive tone and stars a tender fire
And visions rise and change which kill me with desire—

Desire for nothing known in my maturer years
When joy grew mad with awe at counting future tears;
When, if my spirit's sky was full of flashes warm,
I knew not whence they came, from sun or thunderstorm;

But first a hush of peace, a soundless calm descends;
The struggle of distress and fierce impatience ends;
Mute music soothes my breast—unuttered harmony
That I could never dream till earth was lost to me.

Then dawns the Invisible, the Unseen its truth reveals;
My outward sense is gone, my inward essence feels—
Its wings are almost free, its home, its harbour found;
Measuring the gulf it stoops and dares the final bound!

Oh dreadful is the check—intense the agony
When the ear begins to hear and the eye begins to see;
When the pulse begins to throb, the brain to think again;
The soul to feel the flesh and the flesh to feel the chain!

Yet I would lose no sting, would wish no torture less;
The more that anguish racks the earlier it will bless;
And robed in fires of Hell, or bright with heavenly shine
If it but herald Death, the vision is divine!

EMILY BRONTË

INDEX OF TITLES AND FIRST LINES